Be sure what you believe

BE SURE

WHAT YOU BELIEVE

The Christian faith
simply explained

Joe Nesom

EVANGELICAL PRESS

FOUNDERS PRESS

EVANGELICAL PRESS
Grange Close, Faverdale North Industrial Estate, Darlington, DL3
0PH, England

Evangelical Press USA
P. O. Box 84, Auburn, MA 01501, USA

e-mail : sales@evangelical-press.org
web : www.evangelical-press.org

FOUNDERS PRESS
P. O. Box 150931, Cape Coral, FL 33915, U.S.A.

First published 1999

British Library Cataloguing in Publication Data available

ISBN 0 85234 427 9

Printed and bound in Great Britain by Creative Print and Design
Wales, Ebbw Vale

For Janice, Julie and Jaimie

'What you heard from me, keep as the pattern of sound
teaching, with faith and love in Christ Jesus. Guard the good
deposit that was entrusted to you — guard it with the help
of the Holy Spirit who lives in us' (2 Tim. 1:13-14).

'My people are destroyed from lack of knowledge'
(Hosea 4:6).

Contents

Foreword

A friend of mine used to sing a song entitled 'Whad'ya know, Joe?' The answer was:

I don't know nothing;
I ain't foolin',
I need schoolin';
I don't know.

That is not the way that this Joe has to answer. Joe Nesom, the author of this helpful book, brings a wealth of knowledge and experience to the table as he gives loving instruction to those who would eat of the feast of truth he sets before us.

Joe knows the Bible. Every lesson develops a clear biblical theme. He begins with an affirmation of the inspiration of Scripture. Then he demonstrates the importance and authority of that concept as each doctrinal area unfolds in its clearly arranged biblical symmetry. Not only are his Scripture quotations apt and wonderfully adapted to illustrate the point of discussion, the entire fabric of his doctrinal discussion reflects a continual engagement with the story line of the Bible.

Joe knows the confessional history of the church. He maintains a healthy integration of personal biblical exposition and historical awareness of doctrinal development. Orthodox

Christology, formative theological controversies on sin and salvation, evangelical creeds and Baptist confessional history all find their way into his discussion. He doesn't flaunt this awareness as if it were a separate source of authority, but gently weaves it into the narrative at appropriate places like strands of gold that highlight and give pleasant and definable contour to the discussion. The hymns of the church that express the beauty of loved truth give additional historical power to the discussion.

Joe knows the questions and concerns of the laity. The doctrine is profound and historically informed. The biblical content is rich. The advantage also of years of questions from an interested laity gives direction to his discussions. There is something for the one who demonstrates great discernment and has a high passion for knowledge of the truth that leads to godliness. The novice just beginning his pilgrimage is not left behind. Joe plays the role of Faithful, Hopeful and Valiant-for-Truth to the many pilgrims who have asked him for guidance along the way.

Joe knows the rhythm of a pastor's heart. The faces of sheep are on every page. He is an experienced pastor with a record of faithfulness to one congregation for many years. It seems to me that Joe has in mind particular individuals in his congregation that stand in need of just the encouragement, admonition, or exhortation involved in the respective doctrines. He sees lost men and women to whom he has talked and preached; he writes, therefore, that they might feel the importance, the eternal consequences, of dealing honestly with the body of truth he faithfully develops. He urges all who read to make worship of the triune God one of the foremost purposes in their life.

This book can be given to growing Christians and seekers alike. You can have confidence that they will have available food for their souls. Joe's last words of the narrative show both the earnestness of his purpose in this writing and also the sense of stewardship that has driven him to develop a book capable of informing one as to how to answer the question he proposes: 'Dear reader... Are you ready to meet your God?'

Tom J. Nettles
The Southern Baptist Theological Seminary
April 1999

Introduction

In the years just after the resurrection and ascension of our Lord, Jude wrote a short epistle directed against false teachers. He had first intended to write a treatise on the biblical doctrine of salvation, but felt that the need of the hour compelled him to address the subject of the character and goals of those who were maliciously bringing harmful teachings and practices into the life of the church. He told first-century Christians that they should 'contend for the faith that was once for all entrusted to the saints' (Jude 3).

Jude, as well as all of Christ's apostles, taught that there is a body of truth which is given to God's people in the Holy Scriptures. This body of truth, which is the whole counsel of God for his people, must be taught to every generation. It was not so very long ago that thousands upon thousands of children, growing up in Christian homes, used to be catechized concerning the great doctrines of the Bible. Today, the great majority of children who grow up with Christian parents are largely ignorant of the faith.

We also live in a day when the very possibility of knowing absolute truth is questioned or denied. Many professing Christians sound more like Pilate than Christ. They ask, 'What is truth?' (John 18:38), and do not remember that the Lord Jesus Christ had just told Pilate, 'In fact, for this reason I was born, and for this I came into the world, to testify to the truth. Every-one on the side of truth listens to me' (John 18:37).

Christians should have a desire to grow in understanding what the Scriptures teach concerning God, man, sin, salvation and the relationship of the Lord Jesus Christ to all of these areas of truth. They need to study the Bible in order to fam-iliarize themselves with as much of its content as possible. But the goal of this study must not be the winning of arguments, or the mere acquisition of knowledge for its own sake. They need to learn to see how the great doctrines of the faith emerge from the Bible, and how they are intended to shape the lives we live. Christ taught us the importance of loving God with our minds (Luke 10:27). Christians must become thinkers. We must be willing to question the traditions of men and evaluate all teaching and practice in the light of God's Word.

The Lord has not left us alone in this task. If we are truly Christ's servants, we have the Holy Spirit living within us to illumine and to guide us. And the Lord has graciously given to his people men who have the gift of teaching. It is their re-sponsibility to proclaim the truth of God, from age to age.

May we give ourselves wholeheartedly to the task of study, and let us pray that when we hear the Word of God taught, it may take root in our hearts. By that means, we will come to reflect the glory that has been revealed in our Saviour, Jesus Christ. Then we will not fail to learn how to think his thoughts and put them into practice.

1.
God's Word

What is the source of our knowledge of God? For that matter, is there an authority which we can consult that is sufficient to guide us in all matters that concern this life and the next? Indeed there is. The Holy Scriptures provide that guidance for us: 'All Scripture is God-breathed and is useful for teaching, rebuking, correcting and training in righteousness, so that the man of God may be thoroughly equipped for every good work' (2 Tim. 3:16-17).

It is true that there is a revelation of God in nature. God's creative work and his providential guidance of all things give a very clear testimony concerning his existence, his wisdom and his power. This revelation is sufficient to condemn men for their stubborn refusal to acknowledge their need for God. But it is not sufficient to save, or to give us the knowledge that we need to please God in the way we conduct our lives. The testimony of creation can be very impressive. What immense orbits some heavenly visitors have! Comets appear in our skies that last appeared there before the birth of the Saviour, two thousand years ago. How large the purposes of God are! As Paul the apostle taught the church at Rome, such things speak of God's 'invisible qualities — his eternal power and divine nature' (Rom. 1:20). The apostle goes on to say that mankind is without an excuse for not acknowledging the existence of God and the sovereign right that God has to rule his creatures. Such revelations of God as exist in nature and providence are merciful in character.

But it is in the written revelation that the Lord has given us a divinely inspired testimony concerning his way of revealing himself in times past, and particularly concerning the revelation of himself in Christ. We call this written revelation of God's will the 'Bible', or the 'Holy Scriptures'. This collection of divinely inspired books consists of both the Old Testament — that is the Hebrew Scriptures — and the New Testament, which is the testimony of certain divinely ordained men who were used by God to give us an authoritative *word* about our Lord Jesus Christ, and the meaning of his death and resurrection from the dead. It is in the Bible that we discover the truth that we need to know concerning our sins and our present standing before God. It is in the Bible that we discover what God has done for the salvation of undeserving sinners.

The apostle Peter gave testimony concerning the authenticity of the Old Testament when he said, 'For prophecy never had its origin in the will of man, but men spoke from God as they were carried along by the Holy Spirit' (2 Peter 1:21). Notice that Peter identified the Holy Spirit as the true author of Scripture. God was pleased to use human minds and pens to give us the Word of God. But it is truly *God's* Word. Paul put it this way: 'This is what we speak, not in words taught us by human wisdom but in words taught by the Spirit, expressing spiritual truths in spiritual words' (1 Cor. 2:13).

The books of the Bible

The books of what we call the Old Testament were accepted as Scripture by our Lord Jesus Christ. Unlike the Sadducees of his day, who denied the inspiration and authority of much of the Bible, our Lord clearly accepted these books as given to us by God.

After the last of the Old Testament books were written (about 400 years before Christ), Hebrew historians and poets continued to make their contributions to the literature of their day. Many years later in the Christian era these books, that are usually referred to as the Apocrypha, came to be published as a part of some translations of the Bible. These works are valuable for our understanding of the times, but should not be taken for God's own Word. They should not be regarded as authoritative, but should be used as we would any other work of ancient literature.

The New Testament is the collected writings of the men that God used to give us a lasting testimony as to the identity of the Lord Jesus Christ, and to explain to us the meaning of his death on the cross and of his resurrection from the dead. These books also teach us how the Lord fulfilled all of the truths concerning the Messiah's ministry on behalf of sinners. These things had been revealed to God's prophets in Old Testament times.

Taken together, these two great testaments form the Bible, which is God's word to man. It is the written revelation of everything that we need to know in order to find salvation, and of everything that we need to know to live in the way that is pleasing to our God.

The authority of Scripture

But how do we come to know that the Scriptures are actually *authoritative truth* given to us by God? First, we need to know that the Bible is not dependent on the testimony of any human being, of any church, or of scholars. The Word of God is its own testimony. It is self-authenticating. It is the 'living' Word of God which the Lord takes and with it touches our hearts, when we hear it proclaimed and when we read it, or when it is read to us. The apostle John put it this way: 'We accept man's testimony, but God's testimony is greater because it is the testimony of God, which he has given about his Son. Anyone who believes in the Son of God has this testimony in his heart' (1 John 5:9-10).

When the apostle Paul wrote to the church at Thessalonica he reminded them that they had not treated the word from the Lord as just another theory or opinion of man: 'And we also thank God continually because, when you received the word of God, which you heard from us, you accepted it not as the word of men, but as it actually is, the word of God, which is at work in you who believe' (1 Thess. 2:13).

When you and I read a play by a great writer we may say, 'This is truly an inspired work!' But when we talk about the inspiration of the Bible, we are discussing something that is wholly different. We believe, as Christians, that the Bible is the work of God's own Spirit. The Lord used various men to pen the words of Scripture. When we read an epistle of Peter, we can even see Peter's personality expressing itself. The same is true of all the human authors of the Bible. But we also believe, as they did, that the unseen author of all the Scriptures is God. And we believe and teach that the same Holy Spirit who inspired the writers of the Bible comes to our hearts today to be the witness that we need to convince us of the truthfulness of the Word of God.

John spoke about this work of the Spirit in this way: 'But you have an anointing from the Holy One, and all of you know the truth' (1 John 2:20). John could speak in this way because he remembered what the Lord Jesus Christ had taught him while here on the earth: 'But when he, the Spirit of truth, comes, he will guide you into all truth' (John 16:13).

The Bible is God's Word and is wholly true. It must become the only authority for the Christian's life. It must be our *standard*, as it alone has the right to judge all the doctrines and opinions of men. When the Lord Jesus Christ was tempted by Satan to use his divine power to make bread from stones, the Lord replied, 'Man does not live on bread alone, but on every word that comes from the mouth of God' (Matt. 4:4).

Understanding God's Word

Near the end of the last book of the Bible there is a stern word of warning directed towards those who might think that they have the right to add to God's Word, or to take away from it (Rev. 22:18-19). Lost man does not enjoy the 'hard' teachings of God's Word. The perfect righteousness that is described for us in the Scriptures forces us to confront our own sin. The desire to abridge or change the Word of God is a great temptation for those who feel its condemnation.

We have the Spirit of God if we are Christ's. God's own Spirit indwells his people. But this does not mean that we can claim the same ability that the prophets and apostles were given when the Lord used them to write his Word. We do not have inspiration. But we do have illumination. No one will be able really to understand and accept the teachings of the Bible unless the Holy Spirit enables that person to do so (1 Cor. 2:14).

This is true of unbelievers. They need a special work of the Spirit in order to understand what the Bible teaches concerning their alienation from God, and the dangers that await them if they do not repent. The person who has come to know the Lord still needs the illuminating work of God in order to understand and apply the Scriptures. Then we shall be able to use the direct commands of the Lord, found in his Word, to live our lives for his glory. We shall also be able to take the general principles of righteousness that are found in the Bible and apply them to our own lives. We shall need to use the intelligence that the Lord has given us as we trust the Holy Spirit to do his illuminating work.

It is not that the Lord causes us to enter a trance, or to have things revealed in visions, as some did in ancient times. Those things were for that age. But we have a full revelation of God's character and will because of what the Lord Jesus Christ did while here on earth. 'In the past God spoke to our forefathers through the prophets at many times and in various ways, but in these last days he has spoken to us by his Son, whom he appointed heir of all things, and through whom he made the universe' (Heb. 1:1-2). This revelation in Christ is all we need. Our task is to study it, to understand it and to obey it.

We need not think of the Bible as too hard to understand. It is true that there are some passages that are, by their very nature, difficult. This should not surprise us when we consider that it is God, in all of his infinite being, who is the subject matter of the Scriptures. Speaking of the epistles of Paul, the apostle Peter wrote, 'His letters contain some things that are hard to understand, which ignorant and unstable people distort, as they do the other Scriptures, to their own destruction' (2 Peter 3:16).

It is God's purpose, in Scripture, to communicate what we need to know in order to be reconciled to God. Godly men, in past generations, called this the 'perspicuity' of the Bible. These great truths that concern us and our salvation are not difficult to understand. The teaching of Scripture is clear on these things. We might spend a lifetime studying the Word of God, but we can never exhaust its truth or fully master it. Yet a child, using the intelligence that God has given to him, and with the illuminating work of the Spirit, can come to know God.

The law of the LORD is perfect,
    reviving the soul.
The statutes of the LORD are trustworthy,
    making wise the simple

(Ps. 19:7).

The books of the Bible were written in Hebrew (Old Testament) and Greek (New Testament). If we are unable to read those languages, then we obviously need the help of translators. Some translations are better than others. Some do a good job of word-for-word translation, but fail to produce a translation that is true to the language that we speak. Others strive for an understandable result but fail to render the Hebrew or Greek as accurately. Some of the most successful English translations have been the Authorized or King James Version of 1611, the American Standard Version and, most recently, the New International Version. It is often helpful to purchase several good translations of the Bible in one's own language and study them all in order to get a better understanding of the original text.

We must also realize that since the Lord Jesus Christ came to bring the full revelation of God to us, in order to understand the Old Testament, we must read it in the light of its fulfilment in the New Testament. The new will determine the true meaning of the old. The Old Testament is filled with shadows and types (that is, pictorial representations) of our Lord. The New Testament pulls back the curtain and reveals Christ clearly. Then the whole of Scripture becomes a revelation of our God and of what he has done for sinners in Christ. But do not misunderstand: the Old Testament is Scripture in the same sense that the New Testament is; both were directly inspired by God.

Our final authority

Whatever controversy may arise as to what the truth is, or as to what constitutes true practice for Christians, the question must be settled by an appeal to the teaching of the Bible. Tradition will not do. The edicts of church councils may be helpful but are not the final authority. When the apostles tried to convince the people of their day about the truth of salvation through Christ, they did not appeal to such pronouncements. They appealed to the Word of God. When the apostle Paul reached the city of Rome as a prisoner, many people came to hear him, and Luke, the author of Acts, tells us that 'From morning till evening he explained and declared to them the kingdom of God and tried to convince them about Jesus from the Law of Moses and from the Prophets' (Acts 28:23).

The Word of God must be the final judge of all things. Devotional books are flawed. Sunday school publications are not without errors. Works of theology err. Mission publications often unintentionally spread misinformation. Much of what is sold in Christian bookshops is either not very helpful, or so full of bad doctrine as to be virtually useless. But the Bible never fails! Go to God's Word. Read it. Study it. Learn from it before you begin to use the many helpful books that are designed to enhance the study of the Scriptures.

There is also another reason for going to the 'source document', the Bible. C. S. Lewis observed that reading and understanding Plato is much easier than trying to wade through the many works that have been written about Plato. The same thing is true of the Bible. It is true that the Lord has given us pastors and teachers to teach the content of the Scriptures to his church. And good books can be helpful. But that does not mean that a Christian has no need to read his primary textbook, the Bible. Every assertion made in a sermon or in a book should be judged by what the Bible actually says.

Get into the Book of books itself! A true Christian comes to love the Word of God.

> Your statutes are wonderful;
>> therefore I obey them.
> The unfolding of your words gives light;
>> it gives understanding to the simple.
> I open my mouth and pant,
>> longing for your commands
>
> (Ps. 119:129-131).

Questions for discussion

1. What do all people learn about God from the created order? (Rom. 1:18-20).
2. What has God revealed in his Word that cannot be discovered elsewhere? (1 Cor. 2).
3. Who is the true author of the Bible? (2 Peter 1:21; 2 Tim. 3:16).
4. Is it right for us to choose which parts of the Bible we will believe and obey? (Matt. 4:4).
5. What special illumination does one need to understand God's Word? (1 Cor. 2:14).
6. What is the believer's attitude towards the Scriptures? (Ps. 119:129-131).

2.
The living God

God is one. He alone is God. He is the living God, as opposed to the various idols that men fashion for themselves.

Nevertheless, just before the Lord Jesus Christ returned to heaven, he told his disciples to 'Go and make disciples of all nations, baptizing them in the name of the Father and of the Son and of the Holy Spirit' (Matt. 28:19). What can this mean? Why is the name of God threefold?

That God was a Father to his people is one of the most important themes of the Old Testament. The Spirit of God is described as active in the work of creation in Genesis chapter 1. That there is plurality in the Godhead is clear from the language of Genesis 1:26: 'Then God said, "Let us make man in our image, in our likeness."'

This plurality in the Godhead manifests itself, in the progressive revelation given in the Scriptures, as threefold. The Father is God. The Son is God. The Holy Spirit is God. And yet there are not three gods, but only one. Actually, it should not surprise us that God is unlike us in a very fundamental way. We know what it means to be human, and therefore to understand from experience what it is to be one person. But we have no conception from our experience of what it means to be three persons at the same time.

Three persons in one

How can we understand this doctrine of God as triune, as three persons and yet only one God? What troubles us the most? Is it the doctrine that there are three persons in the Godhead? Or is it the teaching that even though there are three persons in the Godhead there is only one God? What is most clearly revealed in Scripture? It is that there are three persons in the Godhead.

Some might reply that the teaching that God is one is clear from the express statements of the Bible. That is true. But we *see* the three persons *more* clearly, in that the Father, Son and the Holy Spirit are all pictured in ways that show all three persons to be fully divine.

An inductive study of the Bible shows us that all three persons are God. Our Lord Jesus Christ, for instance, is portrayed as Jehovah (God's holy name in the Old Testament). Both Matthew and Luke quote an Old Testament prophecy that Jehovah (the LORD) would come to the earth in order to save his people (Isa. 40:1-5), and both Matthew and Luke apply that prophecy to Jesus Christ (Matt. 3:3; Luke 3:4). In other words, both of these New Testament writers regarded our Lord Jesus Christ as Jehovah. They believed him to be the God of Abraham, Isaac and Jacob. John calls Christ the 'Word of God', and he tells us that the Word was God (John 1:1). The writer of Hebrews also ascribes deity to Christ in the first chapter of that epistle.

Would anyone argue that the Holy Spirit is not God? It was the Holy Spirit of God who hovered over the emptiness in anticipation of the words: 'Let there be light' (Gen. 1:2,3). It was God who came to his people on the Day of Pentecost.

That there are three persons in the Godhead is not unclear. The difficulty is in understanding how the three can be one.

How can they have such unity that we must confess that there is only one God? What binds the Father, Son and Holy Spirit together in such a way that, in order to be true to the facts, we must say that they are one?

The Bible teaches us that God is *love* (1 John 4:16). The self-sacrificing love revealed by the cross of Christ is our clue to understanding more about the unity of God. God did not need to create men or angels. He did not need us for companionship. He did not need angels for companionship. God was not lonely. Our God is, within himself, the perfection of love and relationship. What we know as the Trinity is a description of the tri-personal God who made us. We were made in his image and are therefore capable of loving relationships. We need God and we need one another. But God needs no one.

And if that is so, is it not humbling to know that the triune God, who needed none of us, created us, and that he created us even though he knew we would rebel against him and spurn his love? And not only did he create us, but he decided to save us, even though he knew that we would be undeserving sinners, rebels against his righteous will.

In the Bible the three persons of the Trinity are distinguished primarily by their work. Certain activities are ascribed to the Father and other works to the Holy Spirit. This is seen most clearly at the cross. It was the Son, the Second Person of the Godhead, who died for our sins. The Father did not die on the cross, nor did the Holy Spirit. This doctrine of the Trinity is extremely mysterious because it takes us to the very heart of God's being. He is infinite; we are finite. And so, at the boundaries of our finiteness, we find that we can go no further. Only God can fully understand himself: 'In the same way no one knows the thoughts of God except the Spirit of God' (1 Cor. 2:11).

What is God like?

We need to know what our triune God is like. It is only in the Scriptures that his character is revealed in a way that is accessible to us. God is perfectly revealed in our Lord Jesus Christ. And it is in Scripture alone that we have a sufficient and authoritative picture of what God is like, as he has been revealed in Christ.

Anyone can claim to have a personal knowledge of what God is like. But all who profess to know Christ do not agree as to what God is like. There are people who profess to be Christians who teach error concerning the character of God. Their god is not the God revealed in the Bible. He may be the 'man upstairs', or he may be an indulgent father figure who opens the door to the sweetshop and lets us gorge ourselves on the contents. Such a god is hardly the God of Holy Scripture. He is certainly not the true and living God who has come to us in Christ.

The Word of God is our only trustworthy source of information as to the character of God. There we are taught that God is a *Spirit* (John 4:24). The Bible often uses descriptive language when speaking of God such as we would use to describe a man. For example, Proverbs 15:3 tells us, 'The eyes of the LORD are everywhere, keeping watch on the wicked and the good.' But God does not have a body as men do. He does not literally have eyes and ears, or arms and legs. It is only in the person of Christ that God took for himself a human body. God is Spirit and invisible to our eyes.

God is also *eternal*. Our God had no beginning and will have no ending: 'From everlasting to everlasting you are God' (Ps. 90:2).

Only God has *immortality* in and of himself (1 Tim. 6:15-16). It is sometimes said that man's soul is immortal. But

the truth is that we only come to share in the immortal life of
God by faith in Jesus Christ.

God is *infinite*. At times Job's friends were off the mark in
their dialogue with him, but Zophar's question in Job 11:7-8
points to this truth. He asks,

> Can you probe the limits of the Almighty?
> They are higher than the heavens — what can you do?
> They are deeper than the depths of the grave — what
>   can you know?

There are no limits for God. The boundaries that hem us in
cannot hold him.

God is *personal*. He is not a mere power or force that exists as a part of the universe in which we live. He may not be
defined as one would define the law of gravity. He is the living
God who is the greatest of all personal beings. He relates to
mankind and speaks to mankind in a personal way because he
created us as personal beings in his own image.

God is *unchanging* in all that he is. He 'does not change
like shifting shadows' (James 1:17). He is always full of wisdom, and absolute power: 'Great is our Lord and mighty in
power; his understanding has no limit' (Ps. 147:5). The Lord
has always been wholly undefiled by sin and will continue to
be so. The Lord is the fount of true justice and will always be
so. He is good and will always be so. He always was the very
truth itself and always will be so.

God is *holy*. The Hebrew word for 'holy' literally means
'separate'. God is separate from all sin. He has not been de-
filed by sin as we have. But God is also separate in the sense
that he is above all else. He is not dependent on anyone or
anything. Everything depends on him for existence: 'In him
we live and move and have our being' (Acts 17:28).

God is perfect in presence, power and wisdom. The traditional way of expressing these truths is to say that God is

omnipresent — he is everywhere, there is no place where God is not (Ps. 139:7-10); he is *omnipotent* — he has unlimited power to accomplish all his holy will (Job 42:1-2; Isa. 46:8-10); and God is *omniscient* — he sees all; his knowledge is perfect; there is nothing that can be kept from him (Matt. 6:8).

God is *the measure of all things.* He is the one who establishes the standard of justice. It is the commandment of the Lord that is to be obeyed. We must not ask why a thing is righteous apart from its being the will of God. What he has deemed to be right is right (Ps. 119:89-91).

God is also *the absolute ruler of all things,* seen and unseen. This truth does not exclude the possibility of rebellion against his righteous will. Satan is the enemy of God, and so are we until he renews our wills and gives us the ability to love and obey him. But even though he endures rebellion against him for a time, the sovereign will of God will be accomplished at the end, if not before:

> The LORD does whatever pleases him,
>> in the heavens and on the earth,
>> in the seas and all their depths
>
> (Ps. 135:6).

It was to reveal God to us that the Lord Jesus Christ came down to earth. If one wants to know not only what God is like, but to know *him,* one must first know Christ. He is the way, the truth and the life (John 14:6).

'Now to the King eternal, immortal, invisible, the only God, be honour and glory for ever and ever. Amen' (1 Tim. 1:17).

God's purposes

Before anything else came into being God was there. He alone is eternal. He alone has no beginning and no ending. That is a

very strange concept to us. Everything that we experience has
a beginning that we can at least imagine even if we have not
witnessed it — as in the case of a building that is older than
our generation — and we can look forward in time and see the
end of such things by using our imagination. But God is not
like that. He always was, and the Bible teaches us that he was
active before he made the heavens and the earth. Before anything was made, the Lord was planning things that were yet to
come. The Scriptures teach us that God works out everything
in just the way that he chooses. Consider the implications of
Ephesians 1:11: 'In him we were also chosen, having been
predestined according to the plan of him who works out everything in conformity with the purpose of his will.'

Our generation has been greatly influenced by atheism.
Because of that influence many Christians assume that things
often happen for no reason at all. They, thinking like people
who do not know God, believe that we are often subjected to,
and tossed about by troublesome events, simply 'by accident'.
They do not see the hand of God in these things at all. For
them, it is as if there are great areas in their lives that are lived
without any 'input' from the Lord.

But the Bible teaches us that God is never far from us. We
learn from God's Word that he is carefully working out his
purposes. We make decisions. We wonder what the best course
of action is. We wonder if we made the right choice. But in all
of this God is working his purpose out. This began when he
created us, and continues as he providentially guides us every
step of the way, whether we know it or not. But it is far better
to know it. Knowing that God is in control grants us the blessing of living contentedly. No 'accident' will befall us. God
knows what he is doing. That is why the apostle Paul could
say, 'And we know that in all things God works for the good
of those ... who have been called according to his purpose'
(Rom. 8:28).

God made all things and now sustains them. His purposes, that were devised before anything was created, are being brought to pass in the history of this world. Everything that was made and every creature is actually governed by the purposes of God. God is free to do as he pleases. He is able to direct all our paths. Nothing happens by chance: 'The lot is cast into the lap, but its every decision is from the LORD' (Prov. 16:33).

God is not the author of sin. But neither does he simply permit it to take place. There is more to it than that. Even man's fall into sin and the rebellion of some of God's angels have happened in a way that may be said to be according to the purpose of God. He limits and governs even sinful activity so that he is able to turn evil actions to his own purposes. He does not excuse men or angels. But he takes *all* things and works them together for the ultimate good of his own people.

Why, then, do we resist the truth that God has a specific purpose for our lives, and still want to accept that truth when applied to our Lord Jesus Christ? We learn from Scripture that he came to earth because of God's eternal purpose. We learn that he died for precisely the same reason. Peter, on the Day of Pentecost said, 'This man was handed over to you by God's set purpose and foreknowledge; and you, with the help of wicked men, put him to death by nailing him to the cross' (Acts 2:23).

If such trouble came to our Lord (death on the cross), and this was according to God's eternal purpose, why should we not acknowledge that, in the eternal purpose of God, both good things and bad may come our way? And should we not be quick to realize that the same God who raised our Lord Jesus from the dead will grant deliverance to his chosen people? They, after all, are very much a part of his eternal purpose. We are taught in the Scriptures that the centrepiece of God's saving purpose is the creation of a people for himself. He is now working out what the apostle Paul called a 'mystery' that has now been revealed. Paul wrote these words to the church at Ephesus: 'Although I am less than the least of all God's people, this grace was given me: to preach to the Gentiles the unsearchable riches of Christ, and to make plain to everyone the administration of this mystery, which for ages past was kept hidden in God, who created all things. His intent was that now, through the church, the manifold wisdom of God should be made known to the rulers and authorities in the heavenly realms, according to his eternal purpose which he accomplished in Christ Jesus our Lord' (Eph. 3:8-11).

Questions for discussion

1. What is it about God that helps us to understand how the three persons of the Trinity can be but one God? (1 John 4:16).
2. Who alone is immortal? (1 Tim. 6:15-16). What does this tell us about human beings? Can a human being become immortal?
3. What does it mean to say that God is omnipresent, omnipotent and omniscient? (Ps. 139:7-10; Isa. 46:8-10; Matt. 6:8).
4. Does God have a plan for the universe? (Eph. 1:11).
5. What is God doing that causes Christians to be confident of the future? (Rom. 8:28).
6. Who are the witnesses to what God is doing in the working out of his plan for those who believe in Christ? (Eph. 3:8-11; 1 Peter 1:10-12).

3.
All have sinned

What does the Bible teach us about ourselves? How is man portrayed in the Holy Scriptures? Are we the product of chance, or did God create us with a purpose in mind?

Created in God's image

The Bible makes the amazing claim that man is *created in the image of God*. When God made all things he pronounced them 'good', but only mankind is said to have been created in God's very image. We are like God in ways that no other creature can ever be. Even angels, with all their power and splendour, are not said to have been created in the image of God.

Interestingly, there seems to be a connection between man, as male and female, and the image of God:

> So God created man
>   in his own image,
> in the image of God
>   he created him;
> male and female
>   he created them

(Gen. 1:27).

This is a reference to the tri-personal character of our God. Before he made anything, he dwelt in perfect isolation. He alone existed. And yet, within God, there was perfect love, perfect communion among the persons of the Godhead. God did not need us for fellowship. But when the Lord created man, he made him in his image and capable of true fellowship and love. This ability to love is reflective of our Creator's own nature.

The human condition before and after the Fall

When first created, man was without sin, He was flawless in moral rectitude. He had never tasted the wine of disobedience. Not only was he like God in that he bore God's own image, but man had freedom that was God-given. That freedom resembled the freedom that God used in his great work of creation. God is infinite and his freedom to accomplish all his righteous will is without limit. Man was finite as a creature of God, but his freedom was real, none the less.

It is also clear from the account of the creation, and the subsequent fall of mankind into sin, that God gave man sovereignty over all of the created order. The world was ours to use under the over-arching rule of our God. But something tragic took place.

Adam and Eve, the ancestors of everyone who lives on the earth today, were the only human beings ever to live in a state of such extraordinary freedom. But Adam and Eve used their freedom (to choose for or against God's rule over their lives) to disobey. They turned from the commandment of their Creator and sought supposed delights that would in fact only bring them into the realm of suffering and sin.

It is true that Satan instigated this rebellion on the part of man. But Adam and Eve were free to choose for or against God's will. Tempted by the prospect of leaving behind a paradise of innocent fellowship with God and each other, they chose to believe the lie that they could become more like God than they already were as creatures who bore God's own image. And so they ate of the forbidden fruit (Gen. 3:1-6).

The consequence of this initial act of disobedience was cosmic. Gone was the pristine righteousness that Adam and Eve had known which enabled them to have unimpeded fellowship with their God. And they involved the entire human race in their rebellion. Death was the penalty that was attached to sin and that death became the lot of all men. We die physically but first we find ourselves to be dead in sins. We are spiritually dead before God.

And we discover that a spiritual pollution, which Adam and Eve had not known in the Garden of Eden, has touched us in every part of our being. Our nature from conception is spiritually polluted. We are all, by nature, subject to the wrath of God. We all sin inevitably. That is not to say that we are as bad as we could be if we worked harder at disobeying God. We can sink deeper and deeper into the pit of sin. But we are, from birth, rebels against God's holy will.

We are also no longer free in the sense that Adam and Eve knew freedom. We are so touched by sin, and the effect of the fall into sin, that even our wills are enslaved. We find ourselves the subjects of a new master, the devil (Col. 1:13). We are now citizens of the kingdom of darkness. And, without divine intervention, there is nothing that we can do to help ourselves: 'As for you, you were dead in your transgressions and sins, in which you used to live when you followed the ways of this world and of the ruler of the kingdom of the air, the spirit who is now at work in those who are disobedient. All of us also lived among them at one time, gratifying the cravings of our sinful nature and following its desires and thoughts. Like the rest, we were by nature objects of wrath' (Eph. 2:1-3).

Our responsibility

Notice that the apostle identifies our problem as essentially twofold. First, *we are held responsible to God for our sins*. We have sinned. There is no point in trying to avoid responsibility. And because we have sinned, we are due the judgement that sin deserves, which is eternal death. We have been brought before the bar of God's justice. His holy law is the only standard that can be applied there. We have been found utterly lacking. We have no righteousness. No plea can be made to release us. We have not found pardon. We are guilty, and anyone who has seen us can tell that we have been given exactly what we deserve. If sin deserves hell, then we can only say that we deserve to spend eternity there because we have sinned against God and his holy law. When our lives are measured by the Ten Commandments, we discover that we have not loved God with all our heart, soul, mind and strength. We have not loved our neighbour as ourselves. We deserve to die.

Our inability to help ourselves

But there is another part to our 'sin problem'. We are said to be *dead* already. The world has enticed us and we serve, not God, but the ways of this world. The philosophies that motivate the people of this world move us. The world is our master. We do not seek to obey God rather than men. We take our principles for living from the mind of man, not God. We are spiritually dead and enslaved to this world. We do not even have the ability to turn to the Lord until he graciously gives it to us. We are without spiritual life.

There is also the problem of *Satan*. He is the ruler of those who do not know God. We are citizens of his kingdom. It is a kingdom of darkness. He is destruction itself. He hates God and God's creation. But we obey him. We find ourselves en-slaved to him. We are dead to good and alive to evil.

Paul also goes on to say that we have a problem that comes from within. Unlike the world and Satan, who are outside us, this problem is *our own fleshliness*. We have inherited an in-clination to sin from Adam himself. Adam was the head of the entire human race. It is no good to try to claim a personal exemption from this relationship with our father, Adam. Paul even says that we died 'in Adam' (1 Cor. 15:22). When Adam sinned he died spiritually, and with him all of his posterity. Modern man does not do well when it comes to understand-ing our solidarity with others in various relationships. We are very individualistic today. We mostly think in terms of our-selves alone. But the Bible portrays us as one with Adam in sin and death. His sin is our sin, his death our death. We are born as sinners. In a similar way, those who come to faith in Christ are one with him, and therefore his obedience becomes ours; his righteousness becomes ours. Because we are found to be 'in Christ', we are said to be 'alive'.

Since Adam's day all human beings have been sinners from the very point of conception (Ps. 51:5). Every human being who has lived on the face of the earth is a child of Adam. We can all trace our genealogies to him. And from Adam we in-herit the effects of the Fall. We all sin. Have you ever noticed that no one is exempt?

When I was a child, in my first year at school, I rode the city bus to school. My mother gave me the appropriate fare for the trip to school and back. One day a little girl told me that we could go into the corner-shop and spend our bus money on sweets. The problem of riding the bus for free was to be solved by pretending to put money into the receptacle that stood next to the driver's seat.

I was apprehensive at first but after seeing the little girl (whose name was not Eve, but probably should have been) placing her hand over the slot without the driver seeming to notice, I grew very bold indeed. Each day after that, for an entire week, I spent my money on sweets. Each day I pretended to deposit my bus fare. At the end of the week the driver confronted me: 'Joe, you have not put any money in all week long, and neither has that little girl with you!'

I lied: 'Yes, I have, Mr. King!' I was such a convincing liar that I heard two ladies discussing the shameful way the bus driver had treated me.

At a tender age I was already stealing rides from the bus company and then lying to cover it up. Why? What is it about us that causes all little children to sin, almost as soon as they are capable of it? It is the threefold problem that we have inherited from our ancestor. We love the world and hear its voice. We hear and obey the suggestions of Satan. We listen to a darkness from within us and we rush to give in to the lure of the flesh. And we think that we are free. In a sense we are, of course. We freely choose these things because it is our nature to do so.

I have a friend who uses this illustration. You can take an Arkansas buzzard (my friend is from Arkansas) and stake that buzzard out in a Kansas wheat-field. If wheat is all that the buzzard has to eat he will soon die. There is food all around but it is not the nature of a buzzard to eat wheat. If, on the other hand, you provide that buzzard with a stack of dead armadillos, he will survive and flourish. That is a dish to his liking. He will choose to eat dead armadillos.

So it is with us. We freely choose, but only according to our nature. We will always choose the way of the world, the flesh and the devil until God intervenes and changes our nature. Then, and only then, will we choose to humble ourselves before God, and place our faith in Christ alone to save us. Then, and only then, can it be said that God has touched us with his life. We were dead in sins but have been resurrected spiritually by the touch of our God! But until that time we lie before God dead and therefore helpless. We are like the bones in Ezekiel's vision, awaiting the touch of God to bring us to life (Ezek. 37). We do not have the ability to choose God. We will not choose to put our faith in the Lord Jesus Christ until the Lord changes our nature. That is what the Bible calls the new birth, or regeneration. Even after we have been born again there is sin remaining in us (1 John 1:8-10). But after regeneration we have the power of God's own Spirit to oppose the world, the flesh and the devil. Now we hear the voice of God and we have the ability and the desire to obey him.

Good news for sinners

The glorious gospel message is that even though we are sinners, and touched in every part of our being by the ravages of sin, the Lord is still a God of love and mercy. What you and I have no power to do, the Lord can do. He can take sinners and rip them from the clutches of Satan. He finds them dead in their trespasses and sins, and he touches them with the same power that raised our Lord Jesus Christ from the dead. He is faithful to accept every sinner who repents and to forgive all our sins.

In Christ our God restores what was lost in the Fall and more besides. Adam and Eve enjoyed the fellowship of their Creator when he came to visit them in their earthly paradise. We enjoy fellowship with our Creator now, through Christ, and one day we shall know paradise in a renewed heaven and renewed earth. There, with all of the redeemed of all the ages, we shall praise God for all eternity and shall know his intimate loving fellowship, not just in a series of occasional visits, but for all eternity.

The Lord's plan to redeem sinners

Our condition is grave indeed when we are without the Lord and his grace. We are under indictment for our sins. And we are guilty. There is no question about that. It is impossible for anyone to make a good defence before God. Job said long ago:

> But how can a mortal be righteous before God?
> Though one wished to dispute with him,
>   he could not answer him one time out of a thousand
>   (Job 9:2-3).

We are clearly without a workable defence, and our case has been called, but our problem is even greater.

Not only do we have no help from efforts to prove our righteousness, we also discover that we are dead in our sins. We do not even have the ability to turn to the Lord, unless he graciously gives it to us. We are without spiritual life. Like a dead person we cannot help ourselves. All our pretence of being religious (if we have any) is to no avail. Even our good deeds are judged to be like filthy rags in the eyes of God. He demands perfection, and that is what we must have. But we are dead and can do nothing to please the Lord.

Do you understand that every part of our being is touched by sin and death? We are not as bad as we might be; if we work at it, we can get worse. But we are in as bad a state as we can be, short of hell. We are spiritually dead, and it would seem that there is no hope for us.

But the Lord planned to rescue a people for himself long before you and I were born. In eternity past, the Lord decided on a course of redemptive action. It was determined in the eternal counsel of the Father, Son and Holy Spirit that the eternal Son of God, the Second Person of the Trinity, would come to earth at a time chosen by the Father, and live a life of perfect obedience. In order to do this he would accept the humiliation of becoming one of us, a human being. He would take the disgrace of sinners upon himself. In time he would even die the death for sin that was due to us. He would become sin for us. He would take our guilt away by taking it upon himself. The justice of God would be satisfied. The Lord would not excuse sin. He would take the consequences of the sins of his chosen people upon *himself*. He would, on the cross, suffer the hell that was due to us.

The Lord Jesus spoke about his mission in this way: 'And this is the will of him who sent me, that I shall lose none of all that he has given me, but raise them up at the last day. For my Father's will is that everyone who looks to the Son and believes in him shall have eternal life, and I will raise him up at the last day' (John 6:39-40).

What God has done for sinners

Paul, writing to the church at Corinth, said this: 'Now, brothers, I want to remind you of the gospel I preached to you, which you received and on which you have taken your stand... For what I received I passed on to you as of first importance: that Christ died for our sins according to the Scriptures, that he was buried, that he was raised on the third day according to the Scriptures, and that he appeared to Peter, and then to the Twelve...' (1 Cor. 15:1-5).

The gospel of Christ is about what the Lord our God has done for sinners in the history of this world. It is not a mere abstraction. It is not a set of guidelines to help us with our morals. The gospel of Christ is about something that happened. Someone, who was fully man and fully God, died by the hands of Roman executioners, almost two thousand years ago. It is our claim that his death is the fountain-head from which comes the only salvation that any sinner will ever know.

And how do we know that this is true? After suffering on the cross, Christ was placed in a grave that belonged to another man. On the third day something took place that the world had never seen before. He, after bearing our sins, arose from death because it could not hold him. He is alive today. I do not mean that no human being had ever been raised from the dead. Several had been. But this was the first time, and the only time in history, when the Lord God confirmed the truth of what had been accomplished on the cross, by raising our Lord Jesus Christ from death, to die no more. And many people saw him alive, leaving their testimony about this matter for the generations to come.

Do you believe in your heart that Christ truly was resurrected from the dead? Unless the Lord grants the twin graces of repentance and faith, it is not possible to believe (at least in the biblical sense of the word) that the Lord Jesus Christ is alive today. One might consider such a thing a logical possibility, but that is not the same thing as bowing to Christ as Lord by depending upon him to save. The person who 'believes' in that sense knows that he is alive, and that he is our only hope of deliverance from sin and death and hell. Who is able to convince us of something so foreign to our normal experience? Only God can do it.

Questions for discussion

1. What does it mean to say that God created man in his own image? (Gen. 1:27).
2. In the beginning, Adam and Eve only knew God as their master. After the Fall, how did this change? (Col. 1:13).
3. What word does the Bible use to describe our condition as children of Adam and Eve? (Eph. 2:1-3).
4. When does the sin problem begin for us, as individuals? (Ps. 51:5).
5. What has God done to save sinners? (1 Cor. 15:1-5).

4.
Chosen by the Father

We often forget that all three persons of the Trinity are involved in the work of salvation. It is a mistake to talk about the death of our Lord Jesus Christ without attempting to set his atoning work in its eternal context. The Scriptures teach us that the Father chose us, in eternity, before he ever made men or angels. This is called the doctrine of election. The word 'election' literally means 'choice'.

This is one of the doctrines of the Bible that runs against the inclination of human 'wisdom'. It is often opposed by people who profess to know Christ as their Saviour. In the 1800s, J. L. Dagg made this observation: 'The doctrine of election encounters strong opposition in the hearts of men, and it is therefore necessary to examine thoroughly its claim to our belief. As it relates to an act of the divine mind, no proof of its truth can be equal to the testimony of the Scriptures. Let us receive their teachings on the subject without hesitation or distrust; and let us require every preconceived opinion of ours, and all our carnal reasonings, to bow before the authority of God's holy word.'

The scriptural teaching

It is one of the great themes of the Old Testament that God chose Israel from among the nations to be his own people, to have a special relationship to him: 'Blessed is the nation whose God is the LORD, the people he chose for his inheritance' (Ps. 33:12).

That peculiar relationship of God to Israel is a picture of God's spiritual relationship to his church. The church is the 'new' Israel, and she was not chosen in time, but in eternity. Here is how Paul puts it in his letter to the Ephesians: 'Praise be to the God and Father of our Lord Jesus Christ, who has blessed us in the heavenly realms with every spiritual blessing in Christ. For he chose us in him before the creation of the world to be holy and blameless in his sight. In love he predestined us to be adopted as his sons through Jesus Christ, in accordance with his pleasure and will — to the praise of his glorious grace, which he has freely given us in the One he loves' (Eph. 1:3-6).

This choice of God is described as the gift of 'every spiritual blessing'. And we are told that the Father chose us *'before the creation of the world'*. In eternity, before the Lord had created anything, he already knew what he was going to do. And he already knew that our ancestor, Adam, would sin and involve the entire human race in sin and its consequences.

Still, even though he knew what mankind would become, the Lord chose a people for himself. It is also said that his choice of a people to be his own was *'in Christ'*. We were chosen to be saved by the atoning work of the Lord Jesus Christ. He would be the perfect man. He would be without sin. And we would be 'in' him. Our sins would be dealt with by Christ, and this was something that God purposed to do before he made the world. One day this salvation would be worked out on the earth: 'And he made known to us the mystery of his will according to his good pleasure, which he purposed in Christ, to be put into effect when the times will have reached their fulfilment — to bring all things in heaven and on earth together under one head, even Christ' (Eph. 1:9-10).

The goal of this election by the Father is to create a people for himself who are 'holy and blameless' (Eph. 1:4). And that people, we learn from many passages of Scripture, will not be composed only of the chosen people of the Old Testament era (many of whom were rebels against God), but of people from every race and tribe and nation (Rev. 7:9).

This choice of God is *unconditional*. That means that there is nothing that we have done which shows that we deserved to be chosen by the Lord. If someone is choosing members for a baseball team, or for a choir, he will, if he is wise, choose them on the basis of ability. A baseball team with poor players will not achieve the desired results. A choir with members who have no talent, who have no ability to sing, is of no use to anyone. But God's choice is not like that. He did not choose his people because he knew that they would be the best people: 'Brothers, think of what you were when you were called. Not many of you were wise by human standards; not many were influential; not many were of noble birth. But God chose the foolish things of the world to shame the wise; God chose the weak things of the world to shame the strong. He chose the lowly things of this world and the despised things — and the things that are not — to nullify the things that are, so that no one may boast before him' (1 Cor. 1:26-29).

The story of Jacob and Esau illustrates this well (Gen. 27). If I had been given the responsibility of choosing between the two brothers, of picking one of them to receive good things, I would most likely have chosen Esau. He was an industrious and seemingly uncomplicated fellow. He probably was a likeable, good-natured sort of man. His brother Jacob was just the opposite. He, with the help of his mother, tricked Isaac, the father of Jacob and Esau, into giving him the paternal blessing, which normally went to the first-born.

Jacob received what he did not deserve. So it is with us. What we receive through Christ comes even though we did not deserve to have it. It comes in spite of the fact that we deserved hell. It comes because God has given undeserving sinners the glorious gift of eternal life. And the apostle Paul told the church at Rome that Jacob and Esau teach us an important lesson concerning the mercy of God: 'Not only that, but Rebekah's children had one and the same father, our father Isaac. Yet, before the twins were born or had done anything good or bad — in order that God's purpose in election might stand: not by works but by him who calls — she was told, "The older will serve the younger." Just as it is written: "Jacob I loved, but Esau I hated"' (Rom. 9:10-13).

Paul concludes that God is demonstrating his mercy to the undeserving. If we were chosen, not on the basis of our worth or ability, but simply because God purposed to show mercy to us, then *all the credit for our salvation belongs to the Lord*. We share none of it. And that is the point. The Lord did not choose us because he knew that we would love him, when others would not. Often the claim is made that the Lord knew which individuals would choose Christ, and therefore he chose those individuals for salvation. That destroys the truth that the Lord saves the undeserving. If he had not chosen us, we would not have chosen him. John says, 'This is love: not that we loved God, but that he loved us and sent his Son as an atoning sacrifice for our sins' (1 John 4:10).

It is also clear from the Scriptures that *the Lord chose us with a view to saving us, and that without fail*. He would choose certain individuals to be his own. The Lord Jesus Christ would come and atone for their sins on the cross. The Holy Spirit would call them to Christ and they would come. There would be no mere possibility that the Lord would have a people to worship him and to enjoy fellowship with him for all eternity. He would accomplish his purpose. He had chosen his people. They would be saved, all of them. The Lord Jesus Christ said, 'All that the Father gives me will come to me, and whoever comes to me I will never drive away' (John 6:37).

More than two hundred years ago Joseph Hart raised the question as to why people oppose this very important doctrine of the Bible. He wrote a hymn which contains these words:

Election! 'tis a word divine;
For, Lord, I plainly see,
Had not thy choice prevented mine,
I ne'er had chosen thee.

God's choice and our responsibility

An issue that is related to the biblical teaching concerning the Father's work in salvation is that of human responsibility. We have already established the truth that the biblical doctrine of salvation glorifies God alone as the author and finisher of our faith. He need not share his glory with anyone. It was the Father who chose us and set in motion the things that have brought about our deliverance.

Almost invariably some people will say, 'But that's not fair!' They will assert that if God chose certain human beings and certain angels (1 Tim. 5:21), then he has not been fair to the human beings and the angels that he did not choose. In his letter to the church at Rome the apostle Paul mentions this objection and gives his answer to it: 'What then shall we say? Is God unjust? Not at all! For he says to Moses, "I will have mercy on whom I have mercy, and I will have compassion on whom I have compassion." It does not, therefore, depend on man's desire or effort, but on God's mercy. For the Scripture says to Pharaoh: "I raised you up for this very purpose, that I might display my power in you and that my name might be proclaimed in all the earth." Therefore God has mercy on whom he wants to have mercy, and he hardens whom he wants to harden. One of you will say to me: "Then why does God still

blame us?..." But who are you, O man, to talk back to God?'
(Rom. 9:14-20).

The line of reasoning is this: God made us; he can do with
us as he pleases. We are his creatures; it is folly to 'talk back'
to God. But Paul also says that God is not unjust in any of
this. If the Lord merely gave us justice, we would all spend
eternity in the torments of hell. That is what we deserve. It is
the heart of a wilful sinner, who is still very much in rebellion
against the Lord, that wants to insist, 'But I am not really that
bad! In fact, I am really a good person, and I do not deserve
such treatment!' It is not justice that we need, but mercy. And
the same apostle teaches us that God's mercy has appeared in
Christ and is offered to all without discrimination. We may
with confidence say to all men that if they will but repent of
their sins and put their faith in Christ, God will receive them.

A summary of the teaching

So we may summarize what the Bible teaches us about election in this way. God has not left the matter of salvation to the
whims of human decision. He is determined to save a people
for himself. And the Lord chose that people in eternity, even
before he made the worlds. He did not choose us because of
any good that he saw in us. He did not choose us because he
knew that we would choose him and that others would not.
He chose us because of his love and mercy. It had nothing to
do with any merit on our part.

We may also say that, having chosen us, he sent the Lord
Jesus Christ to the earth to die for us. The Scripture says,
'You are to give him the name Jesus, because he will save his
people from their sins' (Matt. 1:21).

It is the death of the Lord on the cross that was the realiz-
ation of the Father's eternal plan. The death of the Lord was

of infinite worth. All who hear the gospel are invited to believe; in fact they are commanded to repent! (Acts 17:30). It is the responsibility of God's people to proclaim the gospel. And it is the responsibility of sinful human beings to believe it.

Questions for discussion

1. Who chose a people for himself and when did he do it? (Eph. 1:3-6).
2. Is it true that God chose only the most noble people to be saved? (1 Cor. 1:26-29).
3. To whom did the Father give his chosen people? (John 6:37).
4. Is God unjust to choose some and pass others by? (Rom. 9:14-24).
5. What is it that the Lord commands us to do? (Acts 17:30).

5.
God with us

Who is the Lord Jesus Christ? There is no question that is more important than this one. To answer correctly, scripturally, is to place your feet on a firm foundation of revealed truth. From that solid ground one may move on to learn more and more about our Lord. It is, after all, knowledge of the Lord Jesus Christ that leads us into a life that pleases him.

Some may protest saying, 'But we are not saved by what we know. Our knowledge of Christ is personal, not intellectual.' It is true that we must have a personal knowledge of him. By faith we come to know him; we do not merely come to know a few facts about him. But if our conception of the Lord's identity does not agree with the revelation of Christ's person in Holy Scripture, that will affect our understanding of everything else. For example, if a person does not believe that Jesus is God, but considers him as only a created being, though perhaps one of great authority and power, that person cannot worship Christ in the way that he deserves to be worshipped. Such a person will always think of the Lord as a lesser being than he actually is and consequently will never be able to have a proper relationship with Christ as Lord and Master.

On this issue hangs the eternal salvation of lost sinners. The historic answer of Christians down through the ages has been that Christ is both God and man. This was the formulation of the Nicene Creed in A.D. 325:

I believe in one God the Father Almighty,
Maker of heaven and earth,
And of all things visible and invisible:
And in one Lord Jesus Christ, the only-begotten Son of
    God,
Begotten of his Father before all worlds;
God of God, Light of Light, very God of very God...

Old Testament appearances of God

Before God called the Israelites out of slavery in Egypt, he first revealed himself in a very special way to Moses. One day, while Moses was tending the flock of his father-in-law, the 'angel of the LORD' (or 'the messenger of Jehovah') appeared to him from within a burning bush. We are told that, on this occasion, God spoke to Moses and revealed himself as the God of Abraham, Isaac and Jacob. The Lord Jehovah commissioned Moses to go and lead the people out of bondage.

Moses asked the Lord:

'Suppose I go to the Israelites and say to them, "The God of your fathers has sent me to you," and they ask me, "What is his name?" Then what shall I tell them?'

God said to Moses, 'I AM WHO I AM. This is what you are to say to the Israelites: "I AM has sent me to you."'

God also said to Moses, 'Say to the Israelites, "The LORD [Hebrew, *Yahweh,* which has often been translated by the English word, Jehovah], the God of your fathers — the God of Abraham, the God of Isaac and the God of Jacob — has sent me to you." This is my name for ever, the name by which I am to be remembered from generation to generation' (Exod. 3:13-15).

This revelation of the sacred name of God (*Yahweh*, or Jehovah) is a key to help us understand what the Bible teaches concerning the person of Christ. The mysterious 'angel of the LORD' appears on several occasions in the Old Testament record. He seems to bear the character of Jehovah God himself. Three 'men' appeared to Abraham to announce the destruction of Sodom. But one of the 'men' spoke to Abraham, as God speaking to one of his creatures (Gen. 18). There are several such 'theophanies' recorded in the Scriptures. In each, God appears in human form and speaks to human beings. These suggest the deity of Christ. They do not explicitly set forth the doctrine, however.

Old Testament prophecies

But the Old Testament prophets anticipated special appearances of the messenger of Jehovah or of Jehovah himself. Malachi put it this way: '"See, I will send my messenger, who will prepare the way before me. Then suddenly the Lord you are seeking will come to his temple; the messenger of the covenant, whom you desire, will come," says the LORD Almighty' (Mal. 3:1).

Isaiah prophesied about a 'voice' that would call out in the desert preparing the way for the LORD:

A voice of one calling:
'In the desert prepare
    the way for the LORD;
make straight in the wilderness
    a highway for our God'

(Isa. 40:3).

Notice that it is the Lord himself who was to come. God would come and visit his people.

The authors of two of the Gospels both quote this passage, treating it as a prophecy about Jesus Christ. Both Matthew (Matt. 3:1-3) and Luke (Luke 3:1-6) identify John the Baptist as the 'voice' who came to prepare the way for the LORD, and the Lord Jesus Christ as the one who came. When Jehovah came to his people, he came as Jesus of Nazareth. The use of this well-known passage in Isaiah by Matthew and Luke is proof that these New Testament writers believed and taught the deity of our Lord. But there are even more direct assertions in the Bible.

New Testament statements

We know that God created all things. Paul, writing to the church at Colosse, said of the Lord Jesus Christ, 'He is the image of the invisible God, the first-born over all creation. For by him all things were created: things in heaven and on earth, visible and invisible, whether thrones or powers or rulers or authorities; all things were created by him and for him' (Col. 1:15-16).

Jesus Christ is revealed to us in the New Testament as the Creator of all things. The writer of Hebrews described him in this way: 'In the past God spoke to our forefathers through the prophets at many times and in various ways, but in these last days he has spoken to us by his Son, whom he appointed heir of all things, and through whom he made the universe' (Heb. 1:1-2).

John, calling Christ 'the Word', said, 'In the beginning was the Word, and the Word was with God, and the Word was God' (John 1:1)

And the author of Hebrews, quoting from Psalm 45, said, 'But about the Son he says, "Your throne, O God, will last for ever and ever"' (Heb. 1:8).

After the resurrection of the Lord, he appeared to his disciples. Thomas was there. He had earlier expressed doubts about the resurrection saying, 'Unless I see the nail marks in his hands and put my finger where the nails were, and put my hand into his side, I will not believe it' (John 20:25). Suddenly the Lord appeared among them, and confronted Thomas with his unbelief. Thomas responded, 'My Lord and my God!' (John 20:28). This was no mere exclamation of surprise. In the twinkling of an eye Thomas came to see the obvious implication of the resurrection: Jesus Christ, his Lord, was also his God!

Christ's own words

But did the Lord himself claim to be God? In a debate with the Pharisees the Lord said of himself, 'You are from below; I am from above. You are of this world; I am not of this world. I told you that you would die in your sins; if you do not believe that I am [the one I claim to be], you will indeed die in your sins' (John 8:23-24). Notice that, in the NIV translation, the words 'the one I claim to be' are bracketed. In other translations, such as the NASV and AV/KJV, you will find text in italics at this point. The brackets or italics indicate that the translators felt the need to include these words to make the English less awkward, but they are not found in the original Greek. Jesus literally said, 'Unless you believe that *I am*, you will indeed die in your sins.'

Remember the revelation of the name of God to Moses: 'I AM WHO I AM.' The sacred name of God, *Yahweh* or Jehovah, speaks of his eternal existence. It means 'I am that I am.' He is the self-existing God. And this was the name of the God of Abraham, Isaac and Jacob, the one true and living God who made all things. Jesus bears that name. The name 'Jesus' means 'Jehovah is salvation.' He was also called 'Immanuel', which means 'God with us' (Matt. 1:23).

The Jews who opposed the Lord understood the claim that he was making about himself. When he told them, 'Before Abraham was born, I am!' (John 8:58), they took up stones to stone him. They intended to put him to death by stoning for claiming to be one with God.

Christ is to be worshipped

The writer of Hebrews says, 'Let all God's angels worship him' (Heb. 1:6) and the apostle Paul calls us to worship him in rhapsodic tones:

And being found in appearance as a man,
   he humbled himself
   and became obedient to death — even death on a
     cross!
Therefore God exalted him to the highest place
   and gave him the name that is above every name,
that at the name of Jesus every knee should bow,
   in heaven and on earth and under the earth,
and every tongue confess that Jesus Christ is Lord,
   to the glory of God the Father
                        (Phil. 2:8-11).

When John fell before the angel, who had been sent to him, he was told, 'Do not do it! I am a fellow-servant with you and with your brothers who hold to the testimony of Jesus. Worship God!' (Rev. 19:10). We must be careful to worship the living God alone. Yet we are commanded to give the honour of worship to the one who died in the place of sinners on the cross. Jesus Christ is worthy of worship. Let us bow before him. He is the Lord from heaven. He is God with us.

Questions for discussion

1. Isaiah the prophet foretold that Jehovah would come to his people one day. Who came? What does this teach us about who Jesus Christ is? (Isa. 40:3, cf. Matt. 3:1-3; Luke 3:1-6).
2. If Jesus Christ created all things (Col. 1:15-16; Heb. 1:1-2), what does this imply concerning his true identity?
3. What did the apostle Paul mean by calling Jesus Christ 'the image of the invisible God'? (Col. 1:15).
4. Is Jesus called 'God' in the Scriptures? (John 20:28; Heb. 1:8).

6.
Man for us

There are three great Christian 'holidays'. Good Friday commemorates the atoning death of our Lord on the cross. Easter celebrates his resurrection from the dead and Christmas has become the traditional observance of the incarnation of Christ.

Usually Christmas is only thought of as the birthday of the Saviour. In the minds of many people, it is a time for mankind to celebrate 'peace on earth' and to try, at least for a few days, to be more civil to other people. This understanding of Christmas falls far short of the truth it represents. The failure of our anti-doctrinal age has even caused some people to think of Christmas as a time to bake a cake and sing, 'Happy birthday, dear Jesus, happy birthday to you!' Such an approach reveals a less than satisfactory understanding of what Christmas means. They do not understand that the Lord's birth was, in many respects, different from ours.

We celebrate our birthdays because we regard our initial appearance in this world as something to be happy about. We celebrate what we have gained. As Christians we celebrate the Lord's birth with joy because we have come to see that his first advent was the fulfilment of Messianic prophecies. We are remembering that Christ came to bring salvation to his people.

The wonder of the incarnation

But the Lord's physical entry into this world was not exactly like ours. Certainly, he was born of a woman, but he had also consciously and deliberately taken upon himself the likeness of sinful human beings. He had identified himself with us, most willingly. The glorious Lord from heaven had clothed himself in humble clothing, and he had done it for our sake (Phil. 2:5-11). We cannot understand the great sense of loss which he must have experienced, when he left the bliss of heaven to come to earth. The Christmas celebration is our celebration. We rejoice that God in Christ was willing to become one of us. We rejoice in his incarnation. He has taken our flesh to himself. He has become one of us.

Who is Jesus Christ? He is the God-man. He, as we have already seen, is God with us. But he is also man for us. Our Lord is the one human being who lived prior to his conception and birth. Influenced by the philosophy of the East, some poets have represented man as living in 'heaven' before birth. William Wordsworth put it this way: 'Trailing clouds of glory, we come from God who is our home.' But is this true? There is no indication that any of us, except the Lord Jesus Christ, ever existed before our present life here on earth. The Bible gives no support to such an idea. But of the Lord Jesus Christ we read, 'He is the image of the invisible God, the first-born over all creation. For by him all things were created: things in heaven and on earth, visible and invisible, whether thrones or powers or rulers or authorities; all things were created by him and for him. He is before all things, and in him all things hold together (Col. 1:15-17).

And so the teaching of the Bible is that the Lord Jesus Christ, the Second Person of the Godhead, God the Son, came down to earth in a most extraordinary way. It is not so much that his *birth* was unusual. It seems clear that the birth of the Lord was much like that of other babies. He came into the world just as you and I did. But his *conception* was unique. He had no human father. Christians who are orthodox in their attitude towards the Scriptures believe in the virgin birth of Christ. But it was his virgin conception that should amaze us. Mary was 'overshadowed' by the Holy Spirit. The Lord Jesus Christ had a human mother, but his Father was the eternal God. His conception was miraculous. He would be unlike any other human being who had ever walked upon the face of the earth. He would leave heavenly splendour in a great plan of redemption. He would be sinless. He would come to do what no human being had ever done. He would obey the will of God fully. And by that obedience he would rescue fallen man.

The meaning of the incarnation

But what does it mean to say that the Lord Jesus became a human being? First, it means that *our Creator has revealed himself most fully by becoming part of his own creation.* God has spoken to us through prophets 'at many times and in various ways', but now he has spoken through his Son (Heb. 1:1-2). This is not to say that we only benefit from the teaching of the Lord Jesus. There is much more. We discover what God is like through the revelation given in the birth, life, ministry and particularly the death and resurrection of the Lord. God has been made known in Christ. His power, justice, purity and love are demonstrated clearly in Christ. And the Bible is the written testimony that these things are so.

When we say that God became man we also mean that *he lived a truly human life among us* and accepted the vicissitudes of our existence here on the earth. When Jesus of Nazareth was born, he had the same requirements that all babies have. He needed to be nursed. He needed to be cared for. He was, as far as we can see, vulnerable. Of course, he also was protected by the providence of God. Herod tried to kill him but was unable to do it. But Christ knew hunger and thirst. He knew what it was to become tired along the way. He did not know the hour of his return. In some sense his knowledge was limited. It is said that he grew in wisdom (Luke 2:52). Here is mystery indeed! God willingly accepted our lot in the person of his Son.

The purpose of the incarnation

But what was the principal purpose of Christ's becoming man? It is this: he came to die. 'Since the children have flesh and blood, he too shared in their humanity so that by his death he might destroy him who holds the power of death — that is, the devil — and free those who all their lives were held in slavery by their fear of death' (Heb. 2:14-15).

Some Christians have mistakenly taught that the Lord came to rule and to reign over an earthly kingdom, but when that purpose was frustrated by the opposition of men, he adopted another plan. He would now die on the cross to redeem sinners. But the Bible makes clear that the cross was *the* plan and that this plan was devised by God before the foundation of the world. Christ came to die in the place of undeserving sinners.

Is the Lord Jesus still man? The apostle Paul says, 'For there is one God and one mediator between God and men, the man Christ Jesus' (1 Tim. 2:5). He is man for us now, and there is every indication in Scripture that he will continue to be man for us for all eternity.

Christ our Lord is fully God and fully man. We do not believe that he is a strange composite of humanity and deity. He is not half God and half man. He is not sometimes God and sometimes changed into man. His person is indivisible. He is always the God-man.

Christ's example to us

Our Lord was willing to suffer disgrace, hardship and finally
death on the cross. We are taught in Scripture that we are to
have the same approach to living our lives in honour of him.
We are taught that our attitude should be the same as that of
our Lord. He, though he was God,

> ...made himself nothing,
>> taking the very nature of a servant,
>> being made in human likeness.
> And being found in appearance as a man,
>> he humbled himself
>> and became obedient to death — even death on a
>> cross!
>
> (Phil. 2:7-8).

This attitude will keep us from being conceited. It will cause
us to avoid selfish ambition. It will cause us to humble ourselves before others, and will enable us to consider them as
better than we are. We will, in imitation of the Christ who
became man for us, be concerned not only about our own
interests but also about the needs of others. We will, with our
Lord, stoop down to wash the feet of our brothers and sisters
in Christ.

Questions for discussion

1. Did the Lord Jesus Christ exist before his birth to Mary? (John
1:1-2,14).
2. Which may be more properly called a miracle — Christ's conception or his birth? (Matt. 1:20-21).
3. Why did the eternal Son of God become a man? (Heb. 2:14-15).
4. Does the manhood of Christ continue today? (1 Tim. 2:5).
5. How will our lives be changed if we imitate Christ in his incarnation? (Phil. 2:7-8).

7.
Why Christ came to earth

Several years ago, I was asked to sit as part of a 'presbytery', or ordination council, for a young man who was about to graduate from a seminary. He had been called to serve a church as pastor. Everyone was invited to ask questions of the candidate, so I asked him, 'What is the gospel?' He seemed to be confused by my question. He wanted to know if I meant one of the four Gospels. I replied, 'They are called Gospels because they contain the gospel of Christ. What is the gospel of Christ?' His answer was very unsatisfactory.

The gospel defined

The gospel of our Lord takes us to the heart of the truth that we have received from God. The word 'gospel' is sometimes translated 'good news' or 'glad tidings'. It is truth from God about something that happened almost two thousand years ago.

Towards the end of his first letter to the church at Corinth, the apostle Paul defines the gospel in this way:

> Now, brothers, I want to remind you of the gospel I preached to you, which you received and on which you

have taken your stand. By this gospel you are saved, if you hold firmly to the word I preached to you. Otherwise, you have believed in vain.

For what I received I passed on to you as of first importance: that Christ died for our sins according to the Scriptures, that he was buried, that he was raised on the third day according to the Scriptures, and that he appeared to Peter, and then to the Twelve. After that, he appeared to more than five hundred of the brothers at the same time, most of whom are still living, though some have fallen asleep. Then he appeared to James, then to all the apostles, and last of all he appeared to me also, as to one abnormally born (1 Cor. 15:1-8).

According to Paul, the gospel is not merely the introduction of a new, and perhaps more insightful, philosophy for living. It is true that Christ came to teach us and that he is our 'Rabbi', but he came to do so much more than that. Occasionally you will hear someone suggest that even if the Lord was not raised from the dead, we would still be able to appreciate, and benefit from, his moral teaching. That cannot be the case. Jesus Christ claimed to be God among us. He prophesied his own death on the cross for sinners. He foretold his resurrection. And he appeared to his apostles after his resurrection, and to others, to confirm that what he had told them he would do, he had in fact accomplished.

The gospel is history. There is a story that must be told. If we do not speak to men and women about the death of the Lord and about his resurrection on the third day, we have not preached the gospel, no matter how many scriptures we may multiply. The gospel is about what God did, once and for all, in human history, to secure the salvation of his people. We must tell the world about the cross of Christ. And we must tell the world about the empty tomb. We must be convinced

ourselves that Christ is alive. We must believe that his death
accomplished redemption for his people, and that his resurrection proves that he is King of kings and Lord of lords.

Christ died for our sins

We must also understand that this 'good news' has for its primary application the removal of sins. Paul says that these events
took place 'for our sins'. There are many benefits that derive
from the atonement of Christ. But the first and greatest blessing is that our sins are pardoned. This is the greatest problem
of the human predicament. The Lord Jesus Christ did not come
primarily to make us wiser, though we receive heavenly wisdom in him. He did not come primarily to give us an example
of the power of self-sacrificing love. He certainly did do that.
But that was not the heart of his mission. No, our Lord came
to be our substitute. He would 'become sin for us' (2 Cor.
5:21; 1 Peter 2:24). He would suffer the punishment that was
due to us for our sinful rebellion against Jehovah God. God's
just wrath towards sin would be visited on Christ. This is surely
something that only the Lord God can understand fully. We
deserved eternal punishment but, in a horrible 'moment' of
time, Christ endured the full fury of that wrath.

Again and again during the years of his public ministry, the
Lord told his disciples that he would go to Jerusalem, that he
would be arrested and that he would suffer humiliation at the
hands of men. He would die a cruel death on an executioner's
cross.

On the day of his crucifixion, at high noon, darkness fell
over the whole area and that darkness lasted for three hours.
At mid-afternoon the Lord cried out, *'Eloi, Eloi, lama
sabachthani?'* (Mark 15:34). This was a cry of agony to his

Father above. It means, 'My God, my God, why have you forsaken me?' Surely the Lord Jesus Christ was experiencing what you and I would have experienced for all eternity, but he was enduring this, not just for one person, but for all who would believe in him. He had willingly become a stench in the nostrils of God for his people's salvation. This alienation from the love of his Father must have been of such intensity that we can only imagine the horror of it. In heaven he had known the love of Father, Son and Holy Spirit. That love which was his within the Godhead was of a purity that is beyond anything we can hope to understand this side of heaven. For the sake of undeserving sinners, Christ, who alone is worthy of such love, was cut off from it. Our Lord endured 'hell' for us. The powers of darkness had done their worst. Even in the dark hour of his death the Lord still kept his faith in his Father's loving purpose. Even when his soul cried out 'Why?' he did not waver. At the end he shouted, 'It is finished' (John 19:30). Indeed, his work of redemption was complete. The enemies of the truth had played into the hands of God.

The plan of God

Preaching to the assembled crowd on the Day of Pentecost, Peter said, 'This man was handed over to you by God's set purpose and foreknowledge; and you, with the help of wicked men, put him to death by nailing him to the cross. But God raised him from the dead, freeing him from the agony of death, because it was impossible for death to keep its hold on him' (Acts 2:23-24).

This death of Christ for sinners was not an accident. It was *the* plan of God. The Lord God will not be an accomplice of sinners. But, in Christ, he has found a way to be 'just and the one who justifies those who have faith in Jesus' (Rom. 3:26).

It is this truth that explains what Paul means when he says that the death of our Lord was 'for our sins' (1 Cor. 15:3).

As we have already said, the cross was a part of God's design for saving his people. It was not an accident. And so Paul reminds us that all of these things happened 'according to the Scriptures'. We can read the Old Testament and find multiple testimonies to the coming of the Saviour and to his atoning death.

After the Lord was raised from death, he appeared to two disciples on the road to Emmaus. He told them that Moses and all the prophets (the Old Testament) spoke about him and about his coming work. Later he appeared to his disciples and said, 'This is what is written: The Christ will suffer and rise from the dead on the third day, and repentance and forgiveness of sins will be preached in his name to all nations, beginning at Jerusalem' (Luke 24:46-47). If you search the Old Testament you will not find those precise words. But this is the cumulative message of the Bible, and this is the message which he commissioned his disciples to take to the world, until the end of the age.

The way opened to God

When the Lord died, the veil that separated the Holy Place from the Holy of Holies in the temple at Jerusalem was torn in two from top to bottom. God's hand had torn it apart, and thus the Lord signified that it is only by Christ's death that sinners may approach God. By faith in him we may enter the very presence of God with a holy boldness. We need not fear because Christ is alive and is ours.

Charles Wesley's words resound with the joy of this truth:

Bold I approach the eternal throne,
And claim the crown through Christ my own.

Before Christ came to earth the world was decidedly pagan. Idol-worship was the norm throughout all the nations. Of this condition the apostle Paul said, 'In the past God overlooked such ignorance, but now he commands all people everywhere to repent. For he has set a day when he will judge the world with justice by the man he has appointed. He has given proof of this to all men by raising him from the dead' (Acts 17:30-31).

The death and resurrection of Christ were the central feature of all the apostolic preaching. A quick survey of the preaching of the apostles as recorded in the book of Acts will reveal this to be true. When Peter preached on the Day of Pentecost, his 'witness' to the people was that the one who had been crucified had in fact been raised to life (Acts 2:22-36). When the Lord's disciples were called before the Sanhedrin the charge made against them was that they were 'proclaiming in Jesus the resurrection of the dead' (Acts 4:2). They were bold to assign guilt to those who had crucified him, and they insisted that salvation could not be found anywhere else (e.g. Acts 3:13-23; 4:10-12; 13:27-39).

We live in a time when the spirit of the age encourages men and women to believe that there are many ways to God. The Christian faith teaches otherwise. Jesus claimed to be the way and the truth and the life. And his apostles and disciples in every age have received him as such. We are called to tell the world that the only hope for sinners to be reconciled to God is found in Christ alone. We must tell the old, old story again and again. Christ has come. Christ has died for sinners. Christ is the living Saviour who offers pardon to all who repent of their sins and believe in him.

Questions for discussion

1. What is the gospel story? (1 Cor. 15:1-8).
2. What does the cry of the Lord from the cross, 'My God, my God, why have you forsaken me?' suggest concerning what our Lord was experiencing, as he died for the sins of his people? (Mark 15:34).
3. Was the death of Christ something that God had planned, or was God caught by surprise? (Acts 2:23-24).
4. Where was the gospel to be preached? What was to be the benefit to those who believe? (Luke 24:46-47).

8.
Christ our Priest

Just before his crucifixion, the Lord prayed that the name of God might be glorified in what he was about to do. God spoke from heaven: 'I have glorified it, and will glorify it again' (John 12:28). The Lord was about to win the victory that would vanquish Satan. He would win that victory by dying on the cross and by being raised from the dead. He would be revealed as the true King of kings.

A similar thing had happened on the mountain when the Lord was revealed in his glory. There the voice had said, 'This is my Son, whom I have chosen; listen to him' (Luke 9:35). From that point on, the Lord's ministry would increasingly reflect that of the prophets who spoke the truth of God in the face of opposition.

But at the beginning of his earthly ministry among us, there was another occasion when the voice of God spoke concerning the Son. John the Baptist had been preaching the kingdom of God and calling for people to repent of their sins. One day the Lord Jesus appeared and requested baptism at the hands of John. John tried to persuade him not to be baptized. He recognized the superiority of Jesus. But the Lord told John that he needed to be baptized in order to 'fulfil all righteousness' (Matt. 3:15).

It was the will of the Father for Christ to come into this world and to identify with sinners. He would accept the sign of the repenting sinner (baptism) even though he did not need to repent. He had never sinned. And yet he, who had taken upon himself the likeness of sinful flesh by becoming a human being, would stand in the place of sinners. He would do this in baptism just as later he would do the same thing when he died on the cross. There he would become 'sin for us' (2 Cor. 5:21).

The ministry of instruction

After his baptism, the Lord began a ministry that is reminiscent of one of the priest's duties under the law of Moses. Just before his death, Moses blessed the tribes of Israel. When he came to Levi, the priestly tribe, he said:

> He teaches your precepts to Jacob
> and your law to Israel.
> He offers incense before you
> and whole burnt offerings on your altar
>
> (Deut. 33:10).

The ministry of the Old Testament priest was one of instruction and sacrifice. It was the responsibility of the priest to teach the people of Israel God's laws. When the priests were unfaithful in this, either by neglect of their duty, or by teaching things that were contrary to the law of God, the nation suffered greatly. Hosea received this word from the Lord in his day:

> My people are destroyed from lack of knowledge.
> Because you have rejected knowledge,
> I also reject you as my priests;
> because you have ignored the law of your God,
> I also will ignore your children
>
> (Hosea 4:6).

And so the Lord Jesus Christ began to teach the people. What we call 'the Sermon on the Mount' (Matt. 5-7) is simply the Lord's proclamation and explanation of the law of God. He had not come to abolish the law or the prophets. He had come to fulfil the law. And he would teach God's precepts in a way that caused the people who heard him to be amazed. He did not teach the law in the same way that their teachers did. He taught as one with authority. In his teaching the Lord called for perfection from mankind: 'Be perfect, therefore, as your heavenly Father is perfect' (Matt. 5:48).

The ministry of sacrifice

God demands perfect obedience. And that constitutes the failure of the human race. Not only have we failed to obey God perfectly, we have gone our own way and made no real effort to love him with all our hearts or to love our neighbours as ourselves. But the Lord Jesus came to do just that. He would be the one human being to keep the law perfectly. And he would be the one and only human being who, by his righteousness, would have the right to offer a sacrifice unlike any that the Old Testament priests had offered. His sacrifice would mean the salvation of the race.

The Old Testament priest had interceded for the people with God. The nation of Israel had been given a priesthood by the Lord. Under the terms of the law, which had been given at Mount Sinai, the family of Aaron, of the tribe of Levi, would serve the people as priests before God. They would offer daily sacrifices for the people. And, on the Day of Atonement (Yom Kippur), the high priest was to enter the Most Holy Place in the tabernacle, and later the temple, in order to make atonement for the sins of the nation. This took place once a year (Lev. 16:11-22).

The distinctive nature of Christ's priesthood

But the New Testament tells us that the priesthood of the Lord
Jesus Christ was not the same as the Levitical priesthood which
Israel had known since their days in the wilderness. According to Hebrews 6:20, our Lord has become 'a high priest for
ever, in the order of Melchizedek'. Who was Melchizedek,
and why was the Lord a priest of that 'order'?

Abraham's nephew Lot often seemed to find himself in difficult circumstances. On one occasion Lot and his family, with
all that he owned, were captured and taken away by the com-
bined forces of a number of kings who had succeeded in con-
quering the cities of Sodom and Gomorrah. Lot had made his
home there and this was not to be the last time that his choice
of a place to live would get him into trouble. Abraham, with
his servants (who apparently made up a sizeable army), pur-
sued Lot's captors, attacked them and rescued Lot and his
family. It was then that a mysterious figure called Melchizedek,
the King of Salem, appeared:

> Then Melchizedek king of Salem brought out bread
> and wine. He was priest of God Most High, and he
> blessed Abram, saying,

> 'Blessed be Abram by God Most High,
>   Creator of heaven and earth.
> And blessed be God Most High,
>   who delivered your enemies into your hand'
>   (Gen. 14:17-20).

Melchizedek's name means 'King of Righteousness' and
he is called the King of Salem *(Shalom)*, or King of Peace.

Our Lord is the 'King of Righteousness' because he alone
among men has kept the law of God perfectly. And our Lord

is the 'Prince of Peace' because he alone has brought reconciliation between God and man by his sacrifice of himself on the cross.

The writer of Hebrews identifies at least five characteristics of our Lord's priesthood that are like that of Melchizedek.

The priesthood of Christ is *eternal*. Aaron and his descendants were priests for as long as they lived. But the Lord Jesus Christ lives for ever. His priesthood will never end (Heb. 7:1-3).

The priesthood of Christ is *superior to the Levitical priesthood*. Abraham had paid to Melchizedek a tenth part of all the plunder taken when he rescued Lot. At that time, Levi, the descendant of Abraham and the head of the priestly tribe, was only a forethought. In a sense Levi, since he was to come from Abraham's loins, paid a tenth part to the greater priest, Melchizedek. And the priesthood of Christ is the priesthood of Melchizedek (Heb. 7:4-10).

The priesthood of Christ *provides perfection*. The Old Testament sacrifices did not make the people righteous before God. Their sins were covered. There was assurance that God would not punish them for their sins. And there was an implicit hope that one day the Lord would come to his people to solve the sin problem and provide a way for them to be regarded as righteous in his sight. But the sacrifice of Christ did introduce a righteousness which no sacrifice before had been able to provide. And that righteousness was one born of perfect obedience to the will of God. Christ had come to bring us God's righteousness. Now sinners, through Christ, could find a place of acceptance in the presence of God. In Christ, they would be given perfection (Heb. 7:11-19).

And in Christ we find a priest who, because he lives for ever, is *able to intercede for us eternally*. The apostle Paul, writing to Timothy, speaks in the present tense of our Lord as interceding for us: 'For there is one God and one mediator between God and men, the man Christ Jesus' (1 Tim. 2:5).

The writer of Hebrews taught the same thing. Christ is alive. His victory over sin and death and hell is ours. He is our great High Priest. Therefore, we who trust in Christ may rest assured that he continually intercedes for us. He will never stop being our security. He will keep us for all time and eternity (Heb. 7:20-25).

And, finally, the Lord's sacrifice is *one that will never need to be repeated.* It was a once-and-for-all sacrifice for sins. During the long history of the Christian church there have been many who have advocated a kind of 'Judaism' concerning the sacrifice of our Lord. They have taught that, although the cross was the fountain-head of all cleansing, we may repeat that sacrifice by offering up the body and blood of Christ again in the observance of Holy Communion. They even insist that we must do this in order to make ourselves righteous in God's sight. This could never be true. Christ's death on the cross is unrepeatable. It was the final and all-sufficient sacrifice for sins: 'Such a high priest meets our need — one who is holy, blameless, pure, set apart from sinners, exalted above the heavens. Unlike the other high priests, he does not need to offer sacrifices day after day, first for his own sins, and then for the sins of the people. He sacrificed for their sins once for all when he offered himself' (Heb. 7:26-27).

This is our salvation, that Christ came to atone for the sins of his people. In the Old Testament the high priest wore a breastplate which contained twelve stones. Those stones represented the twelve tribes of Israel. Thus the high priest wore a symbol that represented all the people of God. By his priestly work, he would intercede with God for each and every one.

Both Priest and sacrifice

The Bible clearly reveals the Lord Jesus Christ to us as our great High Priest. But unlike the priests of old he, paradoxically, is both the priest who offered the sacrifice and he is the sacrifice. When John, the forerunner, saw the Lord coming towards him at the very beginning of Christ's work here on earth, he said, 'Look, the Lamb of God, who takes away the sin of the world!' (John 1:29). This sacrifice of our Lord lies at the heart of all gospel truth. He who was absolutely holy, perfectly righteous, would so identify with us in our sins that he would become a substitute for us. As our substitute he would die accursed upon the tree (Gal. 3:13). Just as the sacrificial animal was understood to take the sins of Israel upon itself, so Christ would take our sins upon himself and die as the Lamb of God. He would offer himself up. And he would be the sacrifice offered. William Cowper, speaking of Christ said:

Dear dying Lamb, thy precious blood
Shall never lose its power,
Till all the ransomed church of God
Be saved to sin no more.

The animal to be sacrificed, under the terms of the law, had to be a lamb without a defect, without a blemish. Peter puts it this way: 'For you know that it was not with perishable things such as silver or gold that you were redeemed from the empty way of life handed down to you from your forefathers, but with the precious blood of Christ, a lamb without blemish or defect. He was chosen before the creation of the world, but was revealed in these last times for your sake' (1 Peter 1:18-20).

Thus it was that the God-man, who alone had the ability to obey God perfectly, came down from heaven to do for us what we could never have done for ourselves.

Isaiah, long before the advent of our Lord, prophesied that the Messiah would suffer death as a sacrificial lamb. He would be 'led like a lamb to the slaughter'. The LORD would lay 'on him the iniquity of us all'. But he would live again to see his 'offspring'. By his death he would 'justify many, and ... bear their iniquities' (Isa. 53). This confidence in the success of the Christ who would come to save his people is reflected in the words of Samuel Stennett:

> What wisdom, majesty and grace
> Through all the gospel shine!
> 'Tis God that speaks, and we confess
> The doctrine most divine.
>
> Down from his shining throne on high
> The Almighty Saviour comes,
> Lays his bright robes of glory by,
> And feeble flesh assumes.
>
> The mighty debt his chosen owed
> Upon the cross he pays;
> Then through the clouds ascends to God,
> 'Midst shouts of loftiest praise.
>
> There he, our great High Priest, appears
> Before his Father's throne;
> There on his breast our name he wears,
> And counts our cause his own.

Questions for discussion

1. What priestly duty did the Lord Jesus Christ fulfil in the Sermon on the Mount? (Matt. 5-7).
2. Which tribe of Israel were the priests taken from? (Deut. 18:1-2).
3. Was the Lord Jesus Christ from the tribe of Levi? (Heb. 7:11-14).
4. How long will the high priesthood of Christ endure? (Heb. 6:20).
5. What unique sacrifice did the Lord Jesus Christ offer as our High Priest? (John 1:29).

9.
Christ our Prophet

Near the end of his life, Moses gave a strict warning to the Israelites concerning the 'dark arts' of sorcery and divination. He warned them to be careful to avoid taking their guidance from such 'prophets'. This was the way of the nations, but Israel was to follow a different course. Moses promised them that the Lord would provide direction for them as he had done before. He also told them that one day the Lord would raise up a very special prophet (Deut. 18:15). All who claimed to be prophets would have to be judged by the standard of infallible fulfilment. If they prophesied that an event would take place which in fact did not take place, they were to be put to death. Such a 'prophet' was clearly not from God.

The Old Testament prophets

There were many prophets in the Old Testament era who were sent by God. They often were opposed by the leaders and people of Israel. The writer of Hebrews tells us that some of them 'faced jeers and flogging, while still others were chained and put in prison. They were stoned; they were sawn in two; they were put to death by the sword' (Heb. 11:36-37).

Why did the Lord continually send man after man to suffer such injustice? The answer clearly lies in the loving and merciful heart of God. The prophets spoke for God. They were to call the people back to God's ways. They were to confront the nation with its failure to keep the commandments of God. They were to call the people to repent of their sins. In a day which was virtually destitute of the Word of God, the prophets were to be shining lights who would point the way by proclaiming the truth of God.

Often these true prophets of God stood alone. In King Ahab's day there was an occasion when only the prophet Micaiah was willing to tell the truth regardless of the consequences for himself. He stood with the Lord when all the other 'prophets' were saying exactly what the king wanted to hear. They were 'yes-men'. God's prophets were never of that sort. They were called to be willing to die for the truth. But even God's true prophets were all sinful men, and often their weakness was seen. After enjoying a glorious victory over the prophets of the god Baal, Elijah became fearful and let the threats of the wicked queen Jezebel overwhelm him. He ran away. He actually left the country because of his fear.

Christ as 'the Prophet' foretold in the Old Testament

The New Testament teaches us that the Lord Jesus Christ came to be the perfect Prophet of God. When John the Baptist began to preach about the coming kingdom of God, a group of priests and Levites was sent from Jerusalem to enquire as to his identity. They asked John if he was the Messiah. He said that he was not. They wanted to know if he was Elijah. The prophet Malachi had foretold the appearance of the prophet Elijah before the coming of the Lord. Then they asked if he was 'the Prophet'. They wondered if he might be claiming to be the very special prophet from God that Moses had fore-told. John denied that he had come to be 'the Prophet' (John 1:19-21). But the Lord Jesus Christ is 'the Prophet' sent from God.

In one of his earliest messages preached to the people of Jerusalem after the ascension of the Lord, Peter preached Christ as the Prophet: 'For Moses said, "The Lord your God will raise up for you a prophet like me from among your own people; you must listen to everything he tells you. Anyone who does not listen to him will be completely cut off from among his people"' (Acts 3:22-23).

It is characteristic of the Old Testament prophets that they were to speak God's truth, and that they were called to be used by God to confront the rebellious nations with that truth. They were not popular men. And among the prophets of the Old Testament era there was none greater than Moses and Elijah.

After the Lord Jesus Christ had enjoyed some early ac-claim, he increasingly began to become an irritant to the reli-gious authorities of the day. He even began to teach his own disciples that his death at the hands of those who opposed him was inevitable. After one such occasion, he took three of his apostles, Peter, James and John, and led them up a high moun-tain (Luke 9:28-36). There on the mountain-top the Lord's clothing became as 'bright as a flash of lightning'. Moses and Elijah appeared with him. These men were prophets to their generations. But they could only speak for God to the people. They had no power to save. Now the Lord would be the Prophet for all generations. Moses, Elijah and our Lord began to discuss the *exodein* (Greek word for 'exodus') that the Lord would 'bring to fulfilment at Jerusalem'. Just as Moses had led the children of Israel out of Egyptian slavery long ago, now the Lord would lead his chosen people out of a worse kind of slavery. He had come to deliver people who were in bondage to Satan, to sin, to death and to hell. He, by his death on the cross and by his resurrection from the dead, would lead them into the light of life. And he would not just save one of the nations, but people from every race and tribe and nation. He would call out a new nation, 'a holy nation', as Peter was to call them later on (1 Peter 2:9). But in order to do that he would have to suffer as no prophet before had ever suffered for the truth of God.

Christ as the Word of God

John, in the first words of his Gospel, tells us that the Lord Jesus Christ is the Word of God. Here is a significant difference between the Old Testament prophet and our Prophet. Not only did the Lord Jesus Christ come to *speak* the truth of God, he came to *be* the truth of God. He described himself in this way: 'I am the way and the truth and the life. No one comes to the Father except through me' (John 14:6).

On the cross the Lord Jesus would speak the greatest truth that has ever been spoken. I do not refer to his words spoken on the cross, as precious as they are. All that the Lord had ever said, all he had taught while here among men, was true. But the greatest truth of all was proclaimed, not by what he said, but by what he did. The Lord Jesus would be both Prophet and the prophetic Word. He would both *speak* the Word and *be* the Word of God to mankind.

On the cross the Lord would take the place of undeserving sinners. In doing this he would speak a word from God and about God that could not begin to be wholly transcribed in words on the printed page. The Bible gives us all the truth about this event that we need in order to be saved and in order to pattern our lives after the self-sacrifice of the Lord. But the word that was spoken that day revealed to mankind, once and for all, the merciful heart of our God. Is God indeed love? The death of the one who was both the Prophet and the Word of God spoken says, 'Yes!' Is God merciful to sinners? The death of our prophet cries out, 'Yes!' Has God done something about our dreadful condition? The cross of our Prophet shouts out, 'Yes!' God has come in the person of the Son and has led his chosen people, those chosen by the Father before the world was made, out of the kingdom of darkness and into the kingdom of his Son. The one who is greater than Moses has come and has led forth his people with songs of salvation. The one who never failed to stand against the Evil One himself, who is greater than Elijah or any of the prophets of old, has come and has instructed us in the character and mercy of God.

Our duty to hear him

By his life and by his death, the Lord Jesus Christ has been revealed as our true Teacher and Guide. His instruction is the light that is to guide our pathway. Such a prophetic light will never grow dim. And we are under the commandment of our God to hear this Prophet. There on the mountain with Moses and Elijah, a voice rang out from heaven: 'This is my Son, whom I have chosen; listen to him' (Luke 9:35).

This voice of our Prophet calls us to repentance and faith in Christ for pardon and justification. When we come to know Christ as our Saviour we discover that the Lord has placed his Spirit in us and has given us a will to obey him. We must not be like the stubborn Israelites who refused to hear the voice of God through their prophets. We must determine to think the thoughts of God as the Lord Jesus Christ teaches us these truths. We must go to the Bible, which reveals the mind of God, and there hear the voice of the true Prophet. The apostle Paul said, 'Do not conform any longer to the pattern of this world, but be transformed by the renewing of your mind. Then you will be able to test and approve what God's will is — his good, pleasing and perfect will' (Rom. 12:2).

Questions for discussion

1. What standard was expected of Israel's prophets? (Deut. 18:14-22).
2. What kind of reception did prophets often endure for the sake of truth? Was this true of Christ? (Heb. 11:36-37). What does this suggest as to the possible response we may have in our efforts to preach the gospel?
3. Which two prophets conversed with Christ on the Mount of Transfiguration, and what did they talk about? Compare the mission of Moses with that of Christ (Luke 9:28-36).
4. The apostle Peter was with Christ on the mountain, and heard the voice of God there. After Christ's death and resurrection, Peter said that the word of the prophets has been affected by those events. In what way is this so? (2 Peter 1:19).

10.
Christ our King

If you had been in Jerusalem during 'Passion Week', you might have heard the shouts of the crowd:

> Hosanna!
> Blessed is he who comes in the name of the Lord!
> Blessed is the coming kingdom of our father David!
> Hosanna in the highest!
>
> (Mark 11:9-10).

The Lord Jesus, heir to David's throne, was riding into Jerusalem in one of the most extraordinary public displays of his ministry. Earlier, he had often commanded his followers to be very discreet concerning his true identity.

When he enquired as to what the people were saying about the matter, the disciples reported that some thought him to be John the Baptist, or Elijah, or perhaps one of the other prophets, now raised from the dead. The Lord then asked Peter, 'But what about you? … Who do you say I am?' (Mark 8:29). Peter responded that he was the Christ — that is, the Messiah. The Lord Jesus quickly warned his disciples not to tell anyone (Mark 8:30).

But now Christ is seen riding into Jerusalem, the royal city, in the manner of Israel's Old Testament monarchs. And even though he had shown great reluctance to reveal himself in this way previously, he is now seen willingly accepting the accolades of the people. What did it all mean?

Before the Israelites entered the land of promise they were warned about the dangers of monarchy. But the appearance of an Israelite monarchy was acknowledged as assured. Moses cautioned them to choose only a fellow Hebrew. The king must not be a foreigner, or seek great wealth for himself, or take foreign wives who might entice him to pagan worship. In fact, he was to be a lifelong student of God's laws, a judge who would rule with a spirit of humility (Deut. 17:14-20).

The story of the Israelite kings reveals numerous departures from the standard of Moses. There were indeed periods of revival, but for the most part the record reveals a sorry history of failure, rebellion against the Lord and abuse of authority. The appearance of prophets like Elijah who were willing to confront wickedness in high places must have stirred hope in the hearts of God's faithful people. Still, again and again the pattern was the same. When would a king reign in righteousness on the throne of David?

The promise of the Messianic king

With the appearance of prophets like Isaiah, Jeremiah, Ezekiel and Daniel came the unfolding of a revelation from the Lord of a glorious future day of blessing for his people. And a central part of that expectation was the appearance of a king who would rule in righteousness. Isaiah 9:6-7 is such a passage:

> For to us a child is born,
>   to us a son is given,
>   and the government will be on his shoulders.

And he will be called
>Wonderful Counsellor, Mighty God,
>Everlasting Father, Prince of Peace.
Of the increase of his government and peace
>there will be no end.
He will reign over David's throne
>and over his kingdom,
establishing and upholding it
>with justice and righteousness
>from that time on and for ever.
The zeal of the LORD Almighty
>will accomplish this.

Notice the elements of this prophecy. The coming king 'is born' — that is he comes to us as man — but he is also described as the 'Mighty God'. He is a ruler who produces peace because he is the 'Prince of Peace' *(Shalom)*. The kings of the earth, and particularly those who had reigned in Judah and Israel, were often overthrown by anarchy and by invasion. The Messiah, however, will bring in an unending kingdom. This ruler, who never fails to obey the will of God, will certainly appear and practise justice for the nation. God guarantees it. God's zeal will make it so.

The same expectation is found in Daniel's vision of the throne of God. After Daniel sees God revealed as seated upon his throne, ready to adjudicate the practices of the nations, there suddenly appears a 'son of man', who is himself granted sovereignty over all the nations: 'In my vision at night I looked, and there before me was one like a son of man, coming with the clouds of heaven. He approached the Ancient of Days and was led into his presence. He was given authority, glory and sovereign power; all peoples, nations and men of every language worshipped him. His dominion is an everlasting dominion that will not pass away, and his kingdom is one that will never be destroyed' (Dan. 7:13-14).

Again similar elements shape the prophetic hope. The Messianic king will be a man, and yet all peoples will worship him. It is God who will bring this astounding thing to pass; it is God who has invested the Messianic king with total sovereignty. He will not merely rule over the nation of Israel but over the whole world. And again, whereas earthly kingdoms come and go, the coming kingdom of God will never be destroyed. There will never be ruins to mark the site of a once glorious fiefdom. This kingdom will be eternal.

Christ identified as the coming king

But just how did the writers of the New Testament see the coming of the Lord Jesus Christ in relation to the Old Testament hope for the establishment of a truly just and universal kingdom? Is there evidence to identify the Lord Jesus as the glorious Son of Man?

When the Lord was born, Magi from the 'east' came seeking the one who was born to be the King of the Jews. King Herod, who himself did not meet the Mosaic qualifications to be king (he was not a Jew but an Edomite), and perhaps overcome by insecurity, or possibly just motivated by the usual antipathy of a ruler to the challenge of a 'usurper', enquired as to the place of the Messiah's birth. Had he been a student of the Scriptures he would have known. Again, he was woefully failing to meet the criterion for one who would rule over Israel.

Herod summoned the religious leaders, who quoted the prophet Micah's identification of Bethlehem as the place from whence would come 'a ruler who will be the shepherd of my people Israel' (Matt. 2:1-6). The emphasis in Micah's prophecy is on Israel, but the appearance of non-Israelite Magi from the east recalls the universalism of Daniel and Isaiah.

In the same way Luke's Gospel records how Mary was told by the angel Gabriel that her son would receive the throne of his father David. Again the primary emphasis is on Christ's right to expect obedience from Israel. It is God who will do it. He gives the throne of David, but it will not disappear again from face of the earth. It will endure: 'He will reign over the house of Jacob for ever; his kingdom will never end' (Luke 1:33).

The placing of these words near the beginning of the Gospels, along with the preaching of John the Baptist and then that of the Lord himself concerning the coming of the kingdom of God, ought to alert us to the importance of this theme. This is true of John's Gospel. After becoming a follower of the Lord, Philip went to Nathanael and announced that the 'one' of whom Moses and the prophets had written had in fact appeared, in the person of Jesus of Nazareth. At first Nathanael was sceptical, but when confronted with the Lord's obvious prior knowledge of him, he declared Jesus to be 'the Son of God ... the King of Israel' (John 1:49).

The Lord did not contradict Nathanael, and it is at that point in the Gospel of John that we hear the Lord himself adding an interesting description of his work as King. Heaven would be opened and the very angels would ascend and descend on the Son of Man. Notice that Christ uses the terminology of Daniel ('Son of Man'), and also that of Jacob's dream (John 1:50-51). As Jacob had seen a stairway bridging the expanse between the dwelling-place of God and that of man, so the Lord Jesus Christ, the glorious Son of Man, would bring in the kingdom of God indeed. And one of the most important aspects of the establishment of that kingdom would be that he, by the exercise of his power, would reveal himself to be the only way to eternal fellowship with God.

Confirmation from heaven

There are three occasions in the Gospel record when a heavenly voice rings out in confirmation of the person and work of
Christ. Two of them we have already noted in previous
chapters.

The first is at the baptism of the Lord, and seems to be a
prelude to a ministry that is 'priestly' in character. The Lord
was about to begin a teaching ministry, such as the Levitical
priests were required to perform. But he would not merely
interpret the law; he would proclaim it in an authoritative way.
Such is the character of the Sermon on the Mount. And he
would not merely pronounce men and women to be 'clean',
that is free of disease, as did the Old Testament priests. Christ,
as the High Priest after the order of Melchizedek, would actually heal them. And Christ would not offer animal sacrifices
that were incapable of taking away sins. He would offer himself as the pure and spotless Lamb of God, by dying on the
cross.

The second time a heavenly voice was heard was when the
Lord took Peter, James and John up the mountain and was
transfigured before them. There he met with the prophets
Moses and Elijah. There they discussed his coming *'exodein'*
at the city of Jerusalem (Luke 9:31). The Authorized Version
translates this as 'his decease'. The NIV and NASV render it
'departure'. The literal meaning of the word *exodein* is 'exodus'. As the prophet Moses led his people out of bondage in
Egypt, so the Lord Jesus, the Prophet who not only speaks
the words of God, but is the Word of God, would soon lead
his people out of bondage to Satan, sin and death. He must be
heard, and therefore the voice says, 'Listen to him!' (Luke
9:35).

It is only in John's Gospel that the account of the third
'word' from heaven is given. And it is a crucial part of the

revelation of Christ as King. A number of people who are described as 'Greeks' were among those who had come to Jerusalem for the Passover. They were probably converts to Judaism and therefore had made the pilgrimage to the temple at Jerusalem. They came to Philip and asked to see Jesus. When the Lord heard that these men were seeking him he began to speak about his coming death and resurrection:

> 'Now my heart is troubled, and what shall I say? "Father, save me from this hour"? No, it was for this very reason I came to this hour. Father, glorify your name!'
>
> Then a voice came from heaven, 'I have glorified it, and will glorify it again.' The crowd that was there and heard it said it had thundered; others said an angel had spoken to him.
>
> Jesus said, 'This voice was for your benefit, not mine. Now is the time for judgement on this world; now the prince of this world will be driven out. But I, when I am lifted up from the earth, will draw all men to myself.' He said this to show the kind of death he was going to die (John 12:27-33).

One of the most important works to be accomplished by the death of the Lord would be the 'driving out' of Satan, the prince of this world. The Lord knew that his mission was nothing less than an invasion of this world in order to defeat Satan. His death on the cross for sinners would be the blow that would break the devil's power. He would foil the purpose of the Evil One by doing precisely what Satan hated most of all. Christ would bring glory and honour to God by saving a people who had been held in the clutches of the devil. They would be set free from the kingdom of darkness and would become citizens of the heavenly kingdom. No longer would their king be the prince of darkness, but they would have for their sovereign the Lord from heaven, Christ Jesus himself. And the Lord would be revealed as the rightful ruler of heaven and earth.

The King and the kingdom

There is a paradox in this doctrine. Not only is the Lord Jesus our King; there is a sense in which he is the embodiment of the kingdom of God itself. The kingdom of God is the realm in which God is obeyed. And, in its highest manifestation, the kingdom of God is where obedience to God is revealed in perfection. We define earthly kingdoms in terms of geography and relative political power. It is true that God's sovereign rule is manifested in many ways. He governs the universe, for example. But when man's sin is in view, the issue is how the rule of God can be restored, in perfection, in the lives of men and women. The essence of a kingdom is that the king is the final authority. He is to be obeyed. People acknowledge that he has the right to rule over them. God our Lord is King over all things. But God is perfect and demands that his kingdom be perfect as well. He calls for perfect, unwavering obedience.

That is precisely what the Lord Jesus Christ came to do. He came to the earth in obedience to the will of God. He lived a life of perfect obedience. He kept all of God's holy laws perfectly. He perfectly loved his Father and he perfectly loved his fellow man. Not one other person can make that claim and prove it to be so. Only Christ was sinless. And when the will of the Father was for the Lord to die in the place of undeserving sinners on the cross, and in so doing to save his chosen people, Christ did not falter. In the garden, just before his arrest and crucifixion, he prayed, 'Father, if you are willing, take this cup from me; yet not my will, but yours be done' (Luke 22:42).

The only place where we may find the kingdom of God perfectly expressed is in the life and death of our Lord Jesus Christ. He has been ruled over by God, without any departure from the will of God. He never sinned. The kingdom of God did come, just as John the Baptist and later the Lord Jesus Christ said that it would. And we must 'see' that kingdom if we are to be saved (John 3:3). We must have Christ's perfect obedience, and that can only come to us by the grace of God. It is God's gift to sinners who repent. His obedience is imputed to us. It becomes ours by faith in Christ and this is the ground of our justification before God. In Christ, we receive what we never could have accomplished ourselves; we are regarded by God as obedient and worthy.

Then, having come to Christ, we are called to live a 'kingdom' life. If the Lord Jesus Christ ruled by loving self-sacrifice, so must we. If the one who had all power used that power to wash his own disciples' feet, so must we. If the kingdom of God is perfectly expressed by the Lord's sacrifice of himself on the cross for the undeserving, then that must be our standard as well. The way God's authority is used is often surprising to men. The Lord taught his disciples that they were being called to be citizens of the heavenly kingdom. Such a kingdom would be very different from the kingdoms of men: 'You know that those who are regarded as rulers of the Gentiles lord it over them, and their high officials exercise authority over them. Not so with you. Instead, whoever wants to become great among you must be your servant, and whoever wants to be first must be slave of all. For even the Son of Man did not come to be served, but to serve, and to give his life as a ransom for many' (Mark 10:42-45).

The Lord Jesus Christ is not only the King of kings (Rev. 19:16), but he is the only perfect manifestation of God's righteous rule in the life of a human being. In that sense, he is the kingdom of God. To be in Christ is to be in the kingdom. To see Christ is to see the kingdom. To have faith in him is to 'rule' with him now as we gain victories over temptation and sin.

But one day, when the Lord our King comes again in heavenly splendour, we shall be made perfect as he is perfect. And in that day we shall know by experience what it means to love God with all our heart and soul and mind and strength, and to do so perfectly. In that day we shall know what it means to be pure and sinless. What a hope is laid up for us in heaven! By faith, we rule with the Lord now. It is said that we are seated with him in heavenly places. This we receive by faith. But one day faith will become sight and we shall see him face to face. We shall behold our God in glorified bodies that are free of the taint of sin. Then we shall truly know what it means to say that Christ our King won a victory by his cross that saved us from sin and death and hell.

Questions for discussion

1. Did Christ present himself to Israel as King? (Mark 11:9-10).
2. From which famous King of Israel was the Lord descended? (Rom. 1:1-4).
3. How was the coming kingdom of the Messiah described by the prophet Daniel? (Dan. 7:13-14).
4. What was the victory of our Lord Jesus Christ that established the kingdom of God and broke satanic power? (John 12:27-33).
5. If Christ 'ruled' by serving his people, what does that say about our responsibility to do the same? (Mark 10:42-45).

11.
Innocent before God

Everything that God has given us in his Word is important.
But the Bible teaching is not all on an even plane. Some doctrines are of greater significance than others. For example, the
Bible records the rebellious behaviour of Israel's kings and
their judgement by God. That is something that is worthy of
our study. We can benefit by considering their sin and avoid-
ing it ourselves. But the death and resurrection of the Messiah, our Lord Jesus Christ, is like a great mountain that towers
above everything else on the landscape. As we have seen, the
apostle Paul calls these events the things of 'first importance'.
He and the other apostles taught that these things were done
'for our sins'. The cross and the empty tomb constitute the
history of what God has done to redeem sinners. The words
'for our sins' take us to the issue of application. How do these
things apply to those who have come to believe in Christ?

A broken law and a gracious promise

Our God is the great Lawgiver. His being is the ground of all
morality, of all righteousness. The psalmist said:

> Blessed are they whose ways are blameless,
>   who walk according to the law of the LORD.

Blessed are they who keep his statutes
    and seek him with all their heart.
They do nothing wrong;
    they walk in his ways.
You have laid down precepts
    that are to be fully obeyed.
Oh, that my ways were steadfast
    in obeying your decrees!
Then I would not be put to shame
    when I consider all your commands

(Ps. 119:1-6).

But we and our ancestors before us have been 'put to shame'. We discover ourselves to be lawbreakers, not law-keepers (Rom, 3:9-20).

Adam and Eve were placed in the Garden of Eden under a covenant of works. God gave them a standard of righteous behaviour to obey and, as long as they were obedient, they enjoyed a paradise which included fellowship with God. They were the only human beings ever to live under such an arrangement. As long as they did not disobey the commandment of God, they lived under the blessing of God. But when they disobeyed everything changed. The account given in the third chapter of Genesis shows us that they felt their guilt, even to the point of trying to cover themselves with an absurd form of clothing. When they sinned they suddenly realized that they were no longer fit to come into the presence of the holy God. They perversely tried to blame anyone and anything, including God, rather than acknowledge their sin. Their quality of life changed radically and they came under the sentence of eternal death.

Even in that dark hour the Lord introduced a gracious promise. He clothed them himself with the skins of animals. The animals died so that Adam and Eve could be clothed by God with garments of his own design. So it was that, in the fulness

of time, the Lord Jesus Christ would die so that we who believe in him might be clothed with his righteousness. Finally,
Adam and Eve were banished from the garden and barred from
the tree of life until the time should come when that tree would
flourish and produce the fruit of 'healing' for the nations. Our
Lord Jesus Christ is the tree of life. He is life itself.

Man's inability to save himself

These things speak about a covenant of grace. Man had demonstrated that he was unable to keep himself in a pure relationship with God. Now, if he is to be saved, he must be
sought out by God's love and grace. But God demands perfection. It will not do for mankind to simply be 'good'. We
must be perfect. Nothing impure can stand in the presence of
the true and living God. To do so would mean certain death.
We are all unrighteous. We have all broken God's holy laws.

In the first part of Paul's letter to the church at Rome he
observes that the whole world is given to various forms of
idolatry. Men create 'gods' to suit themselves. They deny the
power and the divinity of God (and these things are clearly
seen) and so leave themselves without any excuse for their
sinful rebellion against the true God. They thus become idol-
aters. And there are other manifestations of sin. Our sexuality
becomes perverted in various ways. We give in to heterosexual
or homosexual temptation. We become greedy. We envy the
blessings given by God to others. We are filled with hatred
and have murderous thoughts that may in time lead to the very
deed. We repeat slanderous things that we have heard about
other people even when we do not know whether those things
are true or not. Pride and arrogance mark our path. We have
no respect for authority. And we find delight in luring others
to join us in sinning against God (Rom. 1).

How can such people ever hope to find perfect righteousness? How can we become innocent in the sight of God? Even if we were to live from this point on without sinning against the laws of God, we would still have our past record to deal with. And we have inherited from Adam an inclination to sin that guarantees our willingness to serve the world, the desires of our own flesh and the devil himself.

The perfect obedience of Christ

But what if God provided perfect righteousness for us? What if God was willing to give us perfection as a gift? We could never hope to earn it. Our situation is far too desperate. But where could such righteousness be found? Here again is the heart of the gospel. This is why Christ came. The Lord Jesus Christ was perfectly obedient in his incarnation. He did not shirk his responsibility to obey the will of the Father, but left the splendour of heaven and became man. He took upon himself the humiliation of identification with sinners. In this he was obedient.

And, while here on the earth, the Lord lived in perfect obedience to the will of his Father. He said, 'Do not think that I have come to abolish the Law or the Prophets; I have not come to abolish them but to fulfil them' (Matt. 5:17).

Our Lord Jesus Christ was without sin (Heb. 4:15; 7:26). In all the years of his life among us, he never disobeyed his heavenly Father. He loved God with all his heart, soul, mind and strength. He loved his neighbour as himself and never failed in this at any point.

And, above all, the Lord Jesus Christ was perfectly obedient when he died in obedience to the will of his Father above. He prayed in the garden of Gethsemane, 'My Father, if it is possible, may this cup be taken from me. Yet not as I will, but as you will' (Matt. 26:39).

He persevered in obedience all the way through death on the cross. There he became sin for us. He took our punishment upon himself. Christ's obedience is pure and complete. And it is that obedience, that righteousness, which the Lord God offers freely to undeserving sinners!

Christ's righteousness credited to us

If I were to be arrested and brought before a judge for the crime of murder, and if evidence could be produced that would make my guilt clear, the judge might very well sentence me to death. However, if on the night that the sentence was to be carried out, the governor of my state decided to pardon me, I would not be executed. What joy that would be — pardoned! The death sentence removed! But I would still be guilty. No governor could change that. Justification is more than pardon. We are all under the sentence of eternal death because of our sins. We need forgiveness; we need to be pardoned. We *must* have a pardon from God if we are to live eternally. But, in Christ, the Lord has given us much more. He has declared us to be innocent before him. Now God regards us as if we had never sinned at all.

How can this be? It is because God has credited Christ's righteousness to our account. He has removed our sins from us as far as the east is from the west. He has clothed us in the righteousness of Christ: 'Blessed is the man whose sin the Lord will never count against him' (Rom. 4:8).

Before justification came, the law of God was like an accusing finger pointing to our sins. But now we stand before the law as innocent as our Lord Jesus Christ himself (Col. 2:13-14). His righteousness is ours. And, amazing as it may seem, that perfect righteousness has come to us as a gift from God.

Justification by faith

How does God's free gift of justification come to us? The
writer of Hebrews used Noah's experience as an example for
us: 'And without faith it is impossible to please God, because
anyone who comes to him must believe that he exists and that
he rewards those who earnestly seek him. By faith Noah, when
warned about things not yet seen, in holy fear built an ark to
save his family. By his faith he condemned the world and became heir of the righteousness that comes by faith' (Heb.
11:6-7).

Notice two things that are central to this passage. First, if
you do not have faith, you cannot please God. Second, the
righteousness that we need comes by faith. But what is faith?
Often people hold very confused notions of what the Bible
means by 'faith'.

Once while serving as pastor in a large city I received a call
from a young lady who was one of our church members. She
asked me to come and visit her mother. She said that her mother
appeared to be very depressed. I immediately drove to their
house. The mother had recently had surgery; she was a single
parent with several children; the house was a disaster; there
was not much money, and she was clearly 'down'. I tried to
talk with her about her relationship to God. I spoke about
faith in Christ and the essentials of the gospel message. She
only shook her head and said, 'I guess I just don't have enough
faith!'

Finally, perceiving that we were not getting anywhere, I
asked her what she meant by 'faith'. As it turned out, she understood faith to be sheer optimism. She thought that if only
she could somehow believe 'hard enough' that everything
would turn out all right, it would. She would recuperate from
her surgery. She would have all the money she needed. They
would live in better housing, and all would be well. But

somehow she just could not persuade herself to be optimistic about the future, and so she had become depressed. Not only was her understanding of her need mistaken, she also had completely misunderstood what I meant by 'faith'.

This understanding of faith may seem odd to those who know their Bibles, but it is not really far from the way that faith is generally understood in today's world. We are told that we must have faith in people. Or we are told that our nation must have faith in the future. In other words, we must be optimistic.

But biblical faith is something quite different; it always has an object. There is an intellectual aspect. We must believe that God exists. But we must also have confidence in him. We must believe that he has made a way for our sins to be removed. We must believe that Jesus Christ is God's gift of perfect righteousness to undeserving sinners. We must, with our hearts, *depend* on Christ for pardon. We must believe that he alone can make it possible for us to come before God without being condemned for our sins.

One of the ways that the Bible describes faith can be very helpful for us today. We are told that God created the heavens and the earth in six days and rested on the seventh. The writer of Hebrews uses this as an illustration of faith. He says, 'Now we who have believed enter that rest' (Heb. 4:3).

A man may try for years to establish his own righteousness before God. He may be convinced that he deserves to live for ever in heaven. He may think of himself as better than others and worthy of salvation. He may believe that salvation is based on his good works. But when he comes to understand the gospel of grace, he will give up trying to work for salvation. Now he will 'rest' in Christ alone. He will come to see that Christ did the 'work' that we needed by living a life of perfect obedience to God, and by dying a death of perfect obedience as well. He will see that all our righteousness is like a collection of filthy rags in the sight of God (Isa. 64:6). He will see that we need to be clothed in perfect righteousness and that such righteousness can only come from God. He will stop trying to work for his salvation and rest in Christ.

Our Lord was once asked the question: 'What must we do to do the works God requires?' He gave this answer: 'The work of God is this: to believe in the one he has sent' (John 6:28,29).

Our faith must have Jesus Christ for its object. It is the opposite of optimism about ourselves and our ability. It involves a recognition that we are morally bankrupt, and incapable of rescuing ourselves from the penalty for our sin, which is eternal death. We must place our confidence in Christ if we are to be pardoned for our sins

God's Word links repentance with faith. Again and again we are told to repent of our sins and believe in Christ. To repent means to change one's mind and to turn around. It means to do an 'about-face' and thus move in a completely different direction. When a sinner repents he renounces the life of sin and embraces God's way. True faith always has repentance as its corollary. Repentance and faith are like opposite sides of the same coin. If you truly repent of your sins, you will place your faith in Christ. If you truly place your faith in Christ, you will repent of your sins.

The gift of God

God's Word also teaches us that God not only gives us forgiveness in Christ, but that he must give us repentance and faith as well. Faith is the gift of God. The apostle Paul taught that salvation is by grace. Grace means that God has given us a gift that is undeserved. We did not deserve to be forgiven. We do not deserve eternal life. But God has given these things to us.

Someone may say, 'But I chose to believe in Christ when others did not believe!' The apostle's answer is that faith is not from ourselves. It is God's gift (Eph. 2:8-9). We cannot boast about anything (Rom. 3:27-28). God even gave us the ability to repent and believe in Christ. Everything has come from God to us as a free gift.

Martin Luther was used by God to bring reformation to a medieval church that taught a system of righteousness by works. People were told that the saints had accumulated more than enough righteousness for themselves. Other people could tap into that treasury of merit by doing good works. These good works were defined as various religious observances. One might make a pilgrimage to a shrine, or venerate a relic, or spend long hours in repetitious prayer. Martin Luther himself tried the path of works. He became a monk. He spent long hours doing religious duties. He said, 'I was a good monk and followed the rules of my order so strictly that I can say that if ever a monk got to heaven by his good works it was I. All my fellow monks would bear me out. If I had kept on any longer, I should have killed myself with vigils, prayers, reading and other exercises.'

God's righteousness was not understood to be a gift given to the undeserving. The medieval church taught that the biblical phrase 'God's righteousness' was merely the basis for his punishment of sinners. But when Luther and thousands of other churchmen came to see that there is a righteousness which God gives to the undeserving and that it comes by faith in Christ, not by works, they found freedom for the first time. They had been church members, but not Christians. They did not know salvation because they were seeking to achieve it for themselves. Now for the first time they came to believe in Christ as their Lord and Saviour. They came to see that we are helpless before God. They came to see that faith in Christ opens the door to the righteousness of God: 'But now a righteousness from God, apart from law, has been made known, to which the Law and the Prophets testify. This righteousness from God comes through faith in Jesus Christ to all who believe. There is no difference, for all have sinned and fall short of the glory of God, and are justified freely by his grace through the redemption that came by Christ Jesus' (Rom. 3:21-24). As Lidie H. Edmunds wrote:

> My faith has found a resting-place,
> Not in device nor creed:
> I trust the ever-living one.
> His wounds for me shall plead.

Questions for discussion

1. What is God's standard of obedience? How many of his laws are we required to obey? (Ps. 119:1-6, cf. Matt. 5:48).
2. Has Christ kept the law of God? Has any other human being? (Matt. 5:17; Rom. 3:9-20).
3. What was the work of Christ which most fully revealed his persevering obedience to his Father's will? (Matt. 26:39).
4. What is the difference between pardon and justification? (Isa. 55:6-7; Rom. 3:21-24).
5. According to the Lord's own teaching, what must we do to 'do the works God requires'? (John 6:28-29).
6. What activity is essential to 'pleasing God'? (Heb. 11:6-7).
7. Where does faith come from? Do we have a natural ability to believe, or do we receive faith as a gift? (Eph. 2:8-9).

12.
The new birth

During the early ministry of our Lord Jesus Christ, a Pharisee, whose name was Nicodemus, came to the Lord and engaged him in conversation. After Nicodemus had acknowledged that Christ was a true teacher and that he had come from God, the Lord began to speak about the necessity of the new birth. Jesus told Nicodemus, 'I tell you the truth, no one can see the kingdom of God unless he is born again' (John 3:3).

There are two Greek words in this text that can carry a double meaning when translated into English. These two words are usually translated 'born again' but can be rendered as 'begotten' and as 'above'. The phrase could, therefore, be translated this way: 'Unless a man is begotten [that is, given life] from above, he cannot see the kingdom of God.' We must have new life. This new life must come from above, that is, from God. And God must beget this life in us. Without the new birth we cannot see God's kingdom. The Lord Jesus impressed upon Nicodemus the truth that unless God acts to save us, we cannot be saved. He taught Nicodemus that nothing less than our becoming new creatures will do. We cannot see God as we are. There must be a radical change that is described in the Bible as a new birth.

The work of God alone

As we have already seen when we discussed man as a sinner before God, all of us lie dead in our trespasses and sins. Nothing less than the intervention of God can cause us to come to life spiritually. God must do it. And it is the special work of the Spirit of God to come to undeserving sinners and speak the word of life to them.

Nicodemus thought that the Lord was talking about a strange miracle that must take place. Somehow a grown man must return to his mother's womb and be born a second time! Our Lord acknowledged that we must be born of woman (he describes this as being born of 'water' or of the 'flesh'), but he also insisted that we must be born of the Spirit of God.

What can we do to effect this new birth from God? The answer is: 'Nothing!' Books have been written by well-meaning people which claim to instruct people as to *how* to be born again. But if we are to be true to the Word of God, we must acknowledge that we cannot tell anyone how to be born again. That is not what the apostles of Christ did when they evangelized. They never went into a city and announced that 'The Way to be Born Again' would be the subject of the sermon for the day. Instead, they called people to turn from their sins and believe in Christ.

We can certainly tell people how to come to Christ for salvation. They must repent of their sins and put their faith in Christ to save them. But repentance and faith proceed from the new birth. In other words, when a person is born again that person is enabled, by the new life that has been imparted to him or her, to repent and believe in Christ. Repenting and believing are what we do. But the new birth is something that only God can do. And God must do his work first.

The *Westminster Confession* of the Presbyterians and the *1689 Confession* of the Baptists both describe the new birth as the Spirit of God, 'enlightening their minds spiritually and savingly to understand the things of God; taking away their heart of stone, and giving unto them a heart of flesh: renewing their wills, and by his almighty power determining them to that which is good, and effectually drawing them to Jesus Christ: yet so as they come most freely, being made willing by his grace'.

Which comes first — the new birth or repentance?

The order is this: first comes regeneration, or the new birth, by the Spirit; then repentance and faith in Christ come as the result of the work of God. *The Baptist Faith and Message* (the confession of faith of the Southern Baptist Convention) puts it this way: 'Regeneration, or the new birth, is a work of God's grace whereby believers become new creatures in Christ Jesus. It is a change of heart wrought by the Holy Spirit through conviction of sin, to which the sinner responds in repentance toward God and faith in the Lord Jesus Christ. Repentance and faith are inseparable experiences of grace.'

Notice the order again. First there is the new birth. Then repentance and faith appear. They are 'inseparable experiences of grace'. If you have been born again, you will repent. If you have been born again, you will believe in Christ. These things have come to us because of the grace of God. He has given us new life. He has given us the ability to repent when others do not. He has given us faith in Christ when others do not believe in him. On one occasion the Lord even told some of his enemies that the reason why they did not believe in him was because the Father had not enabled them to do so (John 6:60-65).

One might say, 'But I thought that God gives us new life *because* we repent. Isn't repentance the condition for being born again?' Not according to the Lord Jesus Christ. He told Nicodemus, 'The wind blows wherever it pleases. You hear its sound, but you cannot tell where it comes from or where it is going. So it is with everyone born of the Spirit' (John 3:8).

Can you and I control the wind? Do we get up each day and decide how fast the wind will blow, or from what direction it will come? Can we stop a tornado from creating havoc as it passes through a defenceless town? Of course not. The wind blows where it pleases.

Do you see the point that the Lord is making? We cannot control or direct the Spirit of God in his work of imparting new life to sinners. He regenerates. He resurrects to new life. He causes us to be 'born again'. The wind of the Spirit must blow. That is why we pray for the Holy Spirit to come to our friends and relatives who do not know the Lord. We ask God to save them. We know that if they are to come to Christ they must be drawn to him by the work of God. The Lord Jesus said, 'I tell you the truth, whoever hears my word and believes him who sent me has eternal life and will not be condemned; he has crossed over from death to life. I tell you the truth, a time is coming and has now come when the dead will hear the voice of the Son of God and those who hear will live' (John 5:24-25).

The Lord was not speaking about the last day when the dead will be raised from their graves. That is clear because, just after he spoke these words, he began to talk about that day: 'Do not be amazed at this, for a time is coming when all who are in their graves will hear his voice and come out' (John 5:28-29).

The work of the Holy Spirit

We are dead in our sins. We cannot help ourselves. God must come to our rescue. He has done that by sending his Son to die in the place of sinners on the cross. But that atoning work must be applied to us individually, and that is the work of

God's Spirit. The Father chose us in eternity. The Son died for his people in time and history. And the Holy Spirit brings the benefits of Christ's death to us. He brings with him the resurrection life of Christ. With the same power that raised the Lord Jesus Christ from the dead he touches us as we lie spiritually helpless, dead before God. Suddenly we rise from our spiritual grave. We believe the gospel. We believe in Christ. We depend on him to save us.

In our dead state we did not love God. Now we love him because he first loved us. We did not love our fellow man. Now we love even those that we once hated. All this is the miraculous result of the new birth. The Lord has touched us with resurrection power. We are truly alive for the first time. We have been born again!

We must make clear that the Holy Spirit, in accomplishing this work of God, uses *the Word of God*. The preaching of the gospel is an essential part of the Holy Spirit's regenerating work: 'For you have been born again, not of perishable seed, but of imperishable, through the living and enduring word of God'(1 Peter 1:23).

There must be a presentation of the truths of the gospel if a sinner is to come to Christ for salvation. But the external call to receive Christ as Lord and Saviour cannot save if it stands alone. There must also be *an internal work of God*. The Holy Spirit must hover over us as surely as he hovered over the formless void. Just as the voice of God said, 'Let there be light!' so the Holy Spirit brings light to our dark world. He says to each of our dead souls, 'Arise!' It is like the Lord Jesus Christ appearing before the tomb of Lazarus and shouting for the dead man to come forth. And, just as Lazarus was called from death to life by the power of God, so we are raised by God's powerful work for us. But Lazarus died again. Not so with those who are born again. The life that began with the new birth will never end.

Questions for discussion

1. According to the Lord Jesus Christ, in his conversation with Nicodemus, how important is the new birth? (John 3:1-8).
2. Why do we need a new birth? What is our condition before we come to Christ? (John 5:24-25; Eph. 2:1).
3. Can we control this work of the Holy Spirit? (John 3:7-8).
4. What is the role of the Word of God in accomplishing the new birth? (1 Peter 1:23).

13.
Christ's true church

There have been times in the history of Christianity when certain doctrines seem to have exercised the interests of people more than others. The nineteenth century produced many movements that had for their major concern the question: 'What is the true church?' The answers varied greatly.

Writers in the Roman Catholic and Anglican traditions argued that the true church is that church which can trace its origin to the apostles themselves, through the men who were their designated successors. They supposedly held a special authority that was transmitted, in a ritualistic fashion, by ordination. The apostles laid their hands on the next generation of pastors, and they in turn on others, and so on down through the centuries. According to this view, the ministry of those who serve in this line of apostolic succession constitutes the essence of the true church.

In the 1800s others (Alexander Campbell for example) taught that the true church is that church which is organized according to principles which were believed to have been found in the Bible. Such attempts to 'restore' the 'New Testament' church created great havoc among the denominations.

Other 'charismatic' individuals argued that all existing churches are false and that God had called them to start 'the true church'. Many new groups appeared. Joseph Smith taught that he had been entrusted with prophetic revelation and that he was being used to bring back the true church (Mormon) and that all the others were false. He actually introduced doctrines that are heretical and bear little resemblance to Christianity. In the pluralistic environment of nineteenth-century America all sorts of organizations claiming to have the truth arose, and many of them soon passed from the scene. Others remain to the present day, and have made converts to their cause throughout the world.

The history of Christianity reveals a similar pattern. Over the centuries, hundreds of sects have arisen claiming to be the true church. Most of them are now known only to historians.

In spite of these confusing developments the question is still legitimate. What is the true church? And how do we know it to be so? The Word of God must be our guide.

The foundation of the apostles and prophets

First, Christ prophesied that his church would be established in the world. On one occasion the Lord asked his disciples what people were saying about his identity:

'Who do people say the Son of Man is?'

They replied, 'Some say John the Baptist; others say Elijah; and still others, Jeremiah or one of the prophets.'

'But what about you?' he asked. 'Who do you say that I am?'

Simon Peter answered, 'You are the Christ, the Son of the living God.'

Jesus replied, 'Blessed are you, Simon son of Jonah, for this was not revealed to you by man, but by my Father in heaven. And I tell you that you are Peter, and on this rock I will build my church, and the gates of Hades will not overcome it' (Matt. 16:13-18).

There is a play on words here. Peter means 'rock' and the Lord refers to building his church upon a rock. This passage has been used to teach that the church was built on Peter and that the authority which he had was passed on by ordination. Others, in an effort to deny that position, have argued that the 'rock' the Lord was referring to was none other than himself, or perhaps the confession of faith, 'You are the Christ, the Son of the living God.'

But the Word of God gives us a different picture. The church is built on an apostolic foundation. There is truth in saying that the church was built on Peter. However, it was not built on Peter alone but on all of Christ's apostles. Paul, writing to the church at Ephesus, said that the church is 'built on the foundation of the apostles and prophets, with Christ Jesus himself as the chief cornerstone' (Eph. 2:20).

This apostolic and prophetic foundation of the church is clearly a matter of revealed truth. God spoke to apostles and prophets. They in turn wrote the Scriptures. It is this revealed truth of God that undergirds his church. That revelation is, of course, 'in Christ'. He is the living Word of God. And Paul goes on to say that the 'chief cornerstone' is Jesus Christ. Without the Lord Jesus there is no revelation of truth. Without the Lord Jesus there can be no church. It is his death and resurrection from the dead that made the church a reality. Christ came to die in the place of the people that the Father had given to him. He won the victory over sin and death and hell and so secured the salvation of his people. We are taught in both the Old Testament and the New that the Lord died for 'many'. The church is the trophy of Christ's atonement. Samuel Stone said of the church:

> From heaven he came and sought her
> To be his holy bride,
> With his own blood he bought her,
> And for her life he died.

The baptism of the Holy Spirit

We must also point out that the Lord Jesus Christ is at present building his church by the baptism of the Holy Spirit. There is a false teaching that one often runs across in churches today. It teaches that the baptism of the Holy Spirit may or may not follow the new birth. Thus many people seek an experience that is subsequent to salvation and they call this experience the baptism of the Holy Spirit.

But the Word of God teaches us that spiritual baptism is something very different. John the Baptist said of Christ, 'I baptize you with water, but he will baptize you with the Holy Spirit' (Mark 1:8).

When does this work of God take place? The scriptural answer is that Holy Spirit baptism takes place when we are born again. It takes place when we believe in Christ and this has been true in virtually every case. For a very good reason the Holy Spirit did not immediately come on some new believers, in order to create a 'second Pentecost' in Samaria. After that no Jewish Christian could deny that God had called Samaritans as well as Jews to Christ (Acts 8:1-25).

Paul equates being baptized by God's Spirit and 'drinking' of God's Spirit in 1 Corinthians 12:13: 'For we were all baptized by one Spirit into one body — whether Jews or Greeks, slave or free — and we were all given the one Spirit to drink.'

This work of the Spirit comes to those who have faith in Christ. This is what our Lord himself taught: 'On the last and greatest day of the Feast, Jesus stood and said in a loud voice, "If anyone is thirsty, let him come to me and drink. Whoever believes in me, as the Scripture has said, streams of living water will flow from within him." By this he meant the Spirit, whom those who believed in him were later to receive. Up to that time the Spirit had not been given, since Jesus had not yet been glorified' (John 7:37-39).

This 'baptism' of God's Spirit places us (all believers) in the body of Christ. It is not an emotional experience that we work up. It is the work of God. It makes all those who are born again a part of Christ's church.

Who constitutes the true church?

So can we identify the true church with any denomination? If all those who are in Christ's body are in fact born again, it should be clear that no local church or denomination can successfully claim to know that all its adherents are saved. There is ample scriptural evidence to show that the Lord and his apostles taught that not everyone who claims to be a Christian is a child of God.

This church is universal in its composition. As we saw earlier, Daniel had a vision of the throne of God in which he saw 'one like a son of man, coming with the clouds of heaven'. This glorious 'son of man' approached the throne of God and was given 'authority, glory and sovereign power; all peoples, nations and men of every language worshipped him. His dominion is an everlasting dominion that will not pass away, and his kingdom is one that will never be destroyed' (Dan. 7:14).

The same collection of peoples is represented in the vision of John. There, standing before the throne of God, are people who are described as from 'every nation, tribe, people and language' (Rev. 7:9). They are the saved of all the ages. They are the true church.

Questions for discussion

1. Did Christ prophesy that his church would prevail over her enemies, or did he teach that her future is still undetermined? (Matt. 16:13-18).

2. What does it mean to say that the church is built on an apostolic foundation? (Eph. 2:19-20).

3. Should we identify the true church with any particular denomination? If not, why not? (1 Cor. 12:13).

4. How many nations, tribes and language groups are included in Christ's church? (Rev. 7:9).

14.
The minister of the Word

The true church is composed of all who have been born again by the miraculous power of God. Such people seek the fellowship of other believers and are quick to join with them in the worship of God. From the beginning worship has been corporate. We live in a day when individualism is often seen as the highest good. We must 'do it our way'. We must insist on our 'rights'. Such a spirit is not encouraged by the Word of God.

It is true that the Lord saves us as individuals and that as individuals we have every reason to give thanks to him for his mercy. But it is equally true that he saves us to be a part of his people. He expects us to work at this. Our natural tendency is to seek our own interests. The Lord calls us to seek the good of others. And so he places us in the local expression of the church. Here we are to discover what fellowship really means. Here we are to discover what service and love look like. Here we will struggle with the truth that, in a sinful world, not all who say they belong to the Lord really do. Here we will join our hearts and voices in praise to God with brothers and sisters in Christ. It is in the church that we will hear men, who have been chosen by the Lord for the task, teaching the great truths of his Word. We will feed on the Word of God in his church, and in the strength of that food we will go out to serve the cause of Christ.

The church of Christ arises and lives by the preached Word. This is true in three areas of its life. The first is the pastor's responsibility to use his teaching office to build up God's people in righteousness. The second is baptism and the third is communion, or the Lord's Supper. The gospel of Jesus Christ is proclaimed in all three activities.

The importance of the teaching ministry

After the coming of the Holy Spirit at Pentecost, we are told that the church demonstrated certain characteristics that should be true of God's people in every age. First of all, 'They devoted themselves to the apostles' teaching' (Acts 2:42). Without regular instruction from the Bible, God's people will grow weak and ineffective because of their ignorance of God's truth.

It is good to read the Bible at home. It is good to meditate on the things of God in the privacy of our own room. But there is a teaching office that has been set in the church by God. This pastoral office is essential to the well-being of God's church. It is not a vocation that is open to everyone. The apostle James said, 'Not many of you should presume to be teachers, my brothers, because you know that we who teach will be judged more strictly' (James 3:1).

Without the regular proclamation and explanation of the Word of God, by a man whom God has called, there can be no church. This great truth was reclaimed in a dark day (the sixteenth century) by the work of the great Reformers. Even church architecture came to reflect the recovery of the Word of God as foundational to the life of his church. Instead of the altar, the pulpit was placed at the centre of things, in a place of prominence, thus saying symbolically that the Word of God is central in the life of God's people.

Pastors are to be chosen by the church, when there is ample evidence that they have been called by God to their task. They must meet certain qualifications that are found in the Word of God (1 Tim. 3:1-7). Unlike others who serve the church in various ways, they must be 'able to teach'. And they must teach the Word of God. They, in turn, are to be supported by God's people in a generous manner (1 Tim. 5:17-18). If that responsibility of the church is met, they will be free to serve the interests of God's kingdom without distraction. It is a sad commentary on the priority that many congregations give to the ministry of God's Word that they do not provide well for their pastor, even though they find money for a myriad of other 'ministries'.

Illustrations from personal experience

Many years ago I lived in south-east Asia, where I joined a church. It was very good to be with other Christians and to offer 'sacrifices of praise and thanksgiving' to the Lord with them. But something was missing. The preaching did not always ring out with the authority that comes from God's Word. I felt that the 'feast' had not been spread. I often went away with a hunger to understand more of what God had said.

My return to the United States and to the metropolitan Washington area brought me to another congregation. In the first service I attended, there was no effort made to excite people artificially. After prayer and praise, through the singing of several great old hymns of the faith, the pastor stood and called for us to open our Bibles to a chapter in the Gospel of Matthew. When he had finished his sermon, I knew that I had been fed good, nourishing food from the Bible. During the time that I was able to sit under that pastor's ministry my understanding of God, and of his Word, grew as it had not done before. In the past a part of my problem had been that I did not have ears to hear good sermons from God's Word. I had heard them with my physical ears, but not always with the illumination that comes by an obedient faith in Christ. But there were many times, in my life, when the preacher had nothing of value to say, because he only set before me his ideas, and not the words of God.

I now understand that what I was hearing was simply 'old-fashioned' preaching in the tradition of the apostles and their heirs in every age. I had, in the providence of God, been taken to a place where the Word of God was explained in a straight-forward way. There was no suggestion that the pastor or people believed that it needed to be enlivened by anything, or anyone, other than the Holy Spirit of God. This is the ministry that the Levites had in Old Testament times: 'They read from the Book of the Law of God, making it clear and giving the meaning so that the people could understand what was being read' (Neh. 8:8).

How different that experience was from one that my wife and I had when first married! We stopped to worship in a church where the pastor, to his credit, took a text and began to preach. But he only had one point and he illustrated it thirteen times! After the first illustration we were clear about what he had in mind. The remaining twelve just got in the way. Illustrations can be helpful, but the pastor's illustrative work can displace God's Word from the centre of our interest. Even well-intentioned efforts can keep us from having a well-rounded meal from the Word of God.

The pastor's responsibilities

The description of the pastor's work in the Bible is presented in paradoxical language. For example, the pastor is character-ized as 'ruling', or directing affairs, in the body of Christ (1 Tim. 5:17). The writer of Hebrews taught, 'Obey your leaders and submit to their authority. They keep watch over you as men who must give an account. Obey them so that their work will be a joy, not a burden, for that would be of no advantage to you' (Heb. 13:17).

The apostles were the first pastors of the New Testament church. They sought to free themselves from administrative work that would keep them from the ministry of the Word and from prayer (Acts 6:1-7). They knew that the Lord had called them to a work that was first and foremost the proclamation of the Word of God to both the lost and the saved. As they taught the Word of God they 'ruled' the church. In other words, as a pastor teaches the Word of God correctly, all are obligated to obey God's Word and apply it to their lives.

But there have been pastors in every age who have wrongly sought to take powers to themselves that have not been granted to them by the Scriptures. This was a problem in the early church. Peter admonished his 'fellow elders' to 'Be shepherds of God's flock that is under your care, serving as overseers — not because you must, but because you are willing, as God wants you to be; not greedy for money, but eager to serve; not lording it over those entrusted to you, but being examples to the flock. And when the Chief Shepherd appears, you will receive the crown of glory that will never fade away' (1 Peter 5:2-4).

The pastor must teach the doctrines of Christ accurately. He must not compromise the message or dilute it to please men. He must preach what God has given in his Word concerning man, sin, the cross of Christ, the new birth and justification by faith in Christ alone. He must not be a man with a dictatorial spirit, but one who has the Spirit of Christ and who therefore seeks to live as an example of self-sacrificing love on behalf of those for whom Christ died. Pastors are 'under-shepherds' with a derived authority. The Lord of the church is Christ. His will and words are our standard for belief and conduct. The pastor's work is to set before the people the things of Christ, in understandable language. It is to be hoped that they will obey, and thus bring great glory to the God who saved them.

Questions for discussion

1. Was the experience of the first Christians primarily personal or corporate? (Acts 2:42-47).
2. Has God given the church certain men, who are called and equipped to explain God's Word? (1 Tim. 3:1-2; Rom. 12:7).
3. What are pastors required to proclaim and teach? (Neh. 8:8; 2 Tim. 3:16).
4. What is the congregation's responsibility to those whom God has called as pastors? (1 Tim. 5:17-18; Heb. 13:17).
5. What must a pastor's life be like? (1 Peter 5:2-4).

15.
Baptism

The new birth, which brought the life of Christ to us, and with it that work of the Holy Spirit which places us in the body of Christ, comes with the preaching of the Word of God: 'For you have been born again, not of perishable seed, but of imperishable, through the living and enduring word of God' (1 Peter 1:23).

We hear the Word of God; the Holy Spirit convicts us of our sin and of our need for salvation through Christ; and we, by God's grace, are born anew into God's kingdom. We are now citizens of the heavenly kingdom. We are babes in Christ. We, like infants, are not ready to speak with eloquence about the Lord. But through baptism we do speak; in fact we preach the Word of God.

Baptism is the individual's profession of faith in Christ. Coming to Christ for salvation is an individual matter. Many people may have been praying for us. Many may have spoken to us about our need for the Saviour. But they cannot believe for us. You and I must go to Christ in the same way that the tax collector in the temple did long ago. We must cry out to the Lord for mercy and trust him to receive us. No one else can do that for us. Christian parents cannot do it. A pastor cannot do it. We must personally go to Christ. And when we believe, we must then obey the Lord's commandment to be baptized in his name. Just before the Lord returned to heaven, he gave these words of instruction to his disciples: 'Therefore go and make disciples of all the nations, baptizing them in the name of the Father and of the Son and of the Holy Spirit, and teaching them to obey everything I have commanded you. And surely I am with you always, to the very end of the age' (Matt. 28:19-20).

Baptism preaches Christ

There are many things that the Lord instructed his disciples to do while he was here on the earth. Why have Christians always recognized that two 'sacraments' or 'ordinances' stand alone in their significance? What is special about communion and baptism? It is this: both baptism and the Lord's Supper preach the gospel of Christ in a way that nothing else is designed to do.

Baptism gives the individual Christian, who has recently come to faith in Christ, an opportunity to preach Christ as his or her own Saviour. In the earliest days of the faith, believers made their way down into a pool or stream in order to say to the world, 'I believe that Jesus Christ died for me, and that he was buried, and that he was raised from the dead for me.' Thus they preached the gospel without ever audibly speaking a word. When this takes place today, we stand looking on as witnesses. We are able to testify that this person, who is being baptized, is now willing to identify publicly with Christ.

When I lived in the Orient, I soon discovered that pagans understand something of the significance of Christian baptism. They know that it is different from many other activities that Christians may engage in. A young person in the country where I lived could attend a Bible study, or a social gathering with

Christians, without censure from the head of his or her family. But any such young people who were baptized would almost certainly be disowned. By baptism we say to the world that, from this point on, we belong to Jesus Christ. He will be our Lord and Master because he died to take our sins away.

When baptism is practised in the ancient way, by the immersion of the person in water, it is very easy to *see* the gospel. The candidate for baptism goes down into the water as Christ went down into the grave. Thus we say to the world, 'He died for me.' Then the person being baptized comes up out of the water which reminds us visually of our Lord's resurrection from the dead. In this way the gospel is preached in a pictorial way (cf. Rom. 6:1-4). And this, appropriately enough, takes place at the very beginning of our pilgrimage with Christ.

The individual's public profession of faith in Christ

And, just as the baptizing work of the Holy Spirit places us in the body of Christ, which is the true church of the living God, so baptism in water places us in the local expression of the body of Christ. Through baptism we become a part of the people of God here on the earth. Baptism logically must come before anything else. We must identify with God's people by being baptized before we participate in the Lord's Supper. This is because baptism is the individual's profession of faith in Christ.

Churches today often substitute something else for baptism as the profession we must make. People are told to profess Christ by walking down an aisle, or by the act of offering their hand to the minister, or by holding up their hand in a service of worship. But none of these things can qualify as a true public profession of faith in Christ. Only baptism can do that because only it portrays the gospel events of Christ's death, burial and resurrection from the dead.

Baptism does not save

We should never make the mistake of thinking that water baptism as a ritual observance washes our sins away. Peter said that we are 'saved' through baptism (the symbol of salvation is never far removed from the reality itself in Scripture) but is quick to add that he does not mean 'the removal of dirt from the body but the pledge of a good conscience towards God' (1 Peter 3:21). It is the internal work of the Spirit that brings salvation. Baptism is the outward and visible sign of that internal work.

Elements of the church fell into this error in centuries past and it is still with us today. In the Middle Ages many people were taught that an infant's sin could be removed by the water of baptism. The taint of original sin, inherited from Adam, would be taken away. Thus thousands of infants were baptized in order to guarantee that they did not go to hell. According to this view they would only have to fear purgatory. (They would perhaps be there for thousands of years!) But true baptism is not something that we do in order to be saved; it is something that we do because our trust is in the Saviour (Acts 8:35-39).

What about infants?

And what about the baptism of infants? This practice is widespread, and has been so historically. There are many sincere and godly Christians who believe that infant baptism is not only helpful but biblical. I take the opposing view. But let me be quick to say that, whatever our understanding of baptism is, we should embrace as brothers and sisters in Christ those with whom we disagree, when we find that we are agreed concerning who Christ is and concerning what he has done for undeserving sinners. If we agree that salvation is by the grace of God, and that we are justified by faith in Christ alone, we have a foundation for fellowship. When we agree on those things, we can, from that common ground, begin to have meaningful discussion concerning our differences. And that is what I will try to do now.

In one sense we should baptize only infants. I do not mean the little babes lying in their mothers' arms, but those who are truly new born in Christ. It is often said that, as Israel circumcised infants in Old Testament times, so the church should baptize the children of believers, thus bringing them into the family of God. But I believe that there is no biblical authority for this. It is a misunderstanding of the spiritual character of salvation. Just as physical infants were brought into the physical nation of Israel by circumcision, so today spiritual infants are brought into a spiritual kingdom (the church) by the water of baptism. To baptize a baby only leads to a false assurance of salvation. The person may think, 'I have my baptismal certificate; it is my passport to heaven.' Many years ago a friend of mine told me that he had always regarded his baptism as an infant in that way until his true conversion to Christ.

Summary

But whatever else we may say about baptism, it is first of all the individual's opportunity to preach Christ. To all the world he or she says, 'I belong to Jesus Christ. He died to take my sins away, was buried for me, and was raised on the third day for my justification!'

Questions for discussion

1. Who commanded the church to baptize disciples? (Matt. 28:19-20).
2. Even though he or she may not speak in an audible way, what proclamation does the new Christian make by being baptized? (Rom. 6:1-4).
3. Does the act of being baptized guarantee that our sins are washed away? (1 Peter 3:21).
4. Will those who have been saved by Christ desire to be baptized? (Acts 8:35-39).

16.
The Lord's Table

Baptism and communion are often referred to as 'ordinances'. An ordinance is a prescribed ceremony. It is a ritual that the Lord himself commanded us to observe. But the Lord commanded his disciples to do many things. What makes this ceremony special? Why does it, along with baptism, stand in a category by itself?

Let us review some things that are true concerning baptism. First, it is an outward sign of the grace of God within us. Second, it causes us to be identified with the people of God. And third, it is a personal profession of faith in Jesus Christ. It pictures the Lord's death and resurrection.

A corporate profession of faith

The Lord's Table, like baptism, is a profession of faith in Christ, but it belongs to all the saved. It is the profession of faith that we all make together. Paul, the apostle, wrote to the church at Corinth about abuses of the Supper in their congregation. He told them about the revelation from the Lord which he had received concerning the Lord's Table: 'For I received from the Lord what I also passed on to you: The Lord Jesus, on the night he was betrayed, took bread, and when he had given thanks, he broke it and said, "This is my body, which is for you; do this in remembrance of me." In the same way, after supper he took the cup, saying, "This cup is the new covenant in my blood; do this, whenever you drink it, in remembrance of me." For whenever you eat this bread and drink this cup, you proclaim the Lord's death until he comes' (1 Cor. 11:23-26).

The Greek word that is translated 'proclaim' is the same word that, in other places, is translated by the word 'preach'. The individual Christian has the opportunity to preach Christ in baptism. The gathered church has the same opportunity, again and again, in communion. And, just as baptism is an outward sign of God's grace within an individual, the Lord's Table is an outward and visible sign of God's grace within his church as a whole.

A thanksgiving

The Lord's Table, or communion, is also sometimes called a 'Eucharist'. This word signifies 'thanksgiving'. Each Lord's Day that is given to the celebration of communion is a special day of thanksgiving for God's church. We remember the gracious character of the gospel. We remember the greatness of the salvation that the Lord has shown us in Christ and we respond with thanksgiving. Our 'feast' becomes a meal of thanksgiving for all that the Lord is, and for all that the Lord has done for his people by his death and resurrection. This communal experience of the benefits of the gospel is expressed in the Word of God in this way: 'Is not the cup of thanksgiving for which we give thanks a participation in the blood of Christ? And is not the bread that we break a participation in the body of Christ? Because there is one loaf, we, who are many, are one body, for we all partake of the one loaf' (1 Cor. 10:16-17).

The death and resurrection of Christ portrayed

Like baptism, the Lord's Table symbolizes his death and resurrection. This is a little more difficult to see at first. When we are witnesses at a baptism, we *see* the death and resurrection of the Lord. We see the baptismal candidates go *down* into the water and then *emerge from* the water. We see them as they say to us, 'I believe that Jesus Christ died for me, and that he was buried for me, and that he arose for me!' They descend into a watery grave. This provides us with a picture of the descent of our Lord Jesus Christ into death and the grave. They rise from that watery grave just as Christ arose from the dead on the third day.

These same elements are present in the Lord's Supper. There we see before us the body of the Lord symbolized by the bread. And there we also see the blood of the Lord symbolized by the cup that we drink. It is very easy to see the death of the Lord for his church in these symbols. But where is his glorious resurrection from the dead? It is in the participation of the church as she eats the bread and drinks the wine. We are saying to each other, and to all the world, that our Lord died for the sins of his people and that he was raised from the dead. He is alive and therefore able to nourish his people. He is our spiritual food. We, by faith, feast on his body and blood. All the spiritual nourishment that we could ever need is found in Christ. We preach this to the world when we gather around the table of our Lord. Christ is risen! He is risen indeed!

The presence of Christ

The Lord's Supper is not *just* a symbol, however. It is an actual meeting with the risen Lord. When the elements are received by faith there is a special spiritual communion with our

Lord. Some people have taught that the Lord's Supper is purely symbolic, that it is merely a picture of the death and resurrection of the Lord. But can this be true? How can the Supper be *just* a symbol if it is described in Scripture as a communion in the body and blood of the Lord? It is ironic that the same Christian who is quick to acknowledge the presence of the Lord in a worship service, and even in a business meeting of a local church, is also quick to say that the Lord is *not* present in the Supper.

Others have taught that the bread and wine are literally the body and blood of the Lord. By using philosophical categories borrowed from the ancient Greeks, they make the claim that the bread and wine *literally* become the body and blood of Christ and that Christ is thus 'received' when we eat and drink. Thus they teach that we receive Christ through the function of eating. It is true that the Lord taught that we must 'eat' his flesh and 'drink' his blood (John 6:53-58). But in the same passage of Scripture he said, 'The Spirit gives life; the flesh counts for nothing' (John 6:63).

We do not need to see the bread and wine as the literal body and blood of Christ, received in a physical sense, in order to believe that our Lord is present, in a very special way, when we gather around his table. Baptism involves a special manifestation of the presence of the Lord and so does the Supper. Christ comes to his people in a unique way, that has for its focus the gospel events, the death and resurrection of Christ. We remember what he suffered and we remember that he is alive and present among us. Our full hearts look up to him who died that we might live. And we, together with all of God's people, are filled with thanksgiving for what God has given to us in Christ.

The Lord's Supper should be observed with proper reverence (1 Cor. 11:17-34). It is not a meal that is primarily about us. It is not just to be observed as we would an opportunity to get together with friends. We do that, but the Lord's Supper is primarily about the glory of God revealed, two thousand years ago, in the death and resurrection of our Lord.

Who is to take part?

Who is invited to participate in the Supper? The biblical answer is that the Lord's Table is only for baptized Christians. Jesus Christ served the Supper to his professing baptized disciples. Every time there is a record of the Lord's Supper in the New Testament the same thing is true (Acts 2:38-42; 20:5-7; 1 Cor. 11:17-28; 12:13). All of these people had professed Jesus to be their Lord, they were baptized, and only then were they admitted to the Supper. We must issue a gentle warning to parents of unbaptized children. Do not allow your child to partake of the Supper and so bring the Lord's displeasure on yourselves.

We must also say that those who profess Christ but who are living in an immoral and unrepentant way should not participate (1 Cor. 5:9-11). The discipline which Christ requires of his church is closely associated with communion. For almost a century there has been a decline in the willingness of churches to practise biblical church discipline. There are thousands of professing Christians who are regarded as members in good standing even though they are known to be wilfully violating the laws of God. Their continual pattern of behaviour raises the question of whether or not their 'faith' in Christ is authentic. Our Lord taught that many would claim to know him as Lord, even though he never knew them as his own.

It is scandalous to realize that it is easier to remain a member of most evangelical churches than to remain a member of a civic club or fraternal organization. We need to reclaim membership integrity in our day, if we truly love the souls of those who bring dishonour to Christ (cf. 1 Cor. 5). Those who live in a fashion that is not worthy of the gospel of Christ need to feel the censure of the church. God's Spirit uses such discipline to touch the consciences of lost people who have made false professions of faith in Christ.

And when the church refuses to have table fellowship with those who do know Christ, but have brought dishonour to him and to his church, the Lord uses that action to cause them to repent of their sins, and seek the fellowship of his people again. Those who see the Lord's Table as an opportunity to indulge the flesh (not seeing the body of Christ at the heart of the observance) and who are unloving and intolerant towards others in the body of Christ, need to examine themselves and repent of all such things before approaching the table of the Lord (1 Cor. 11:27-32).

A means of grace

The grace of God is indeed given to us in baptism and in communion. But God's grace is not received in a mechanistic way. We do not receive the grace of Christ simply *because* we enter the waters or eat and drink Christ's spiritual meal. We were saved by the death of our Lord on the cross and by his true resurrection from the dead. But the Lord's Table and baptism are special means of grace, designed to help us live lives that are worthy of the gospel of Christ.

Long ago, a great Puritan writer described the Lord's Table in this way:

> God of all good,
> I bless thee for the means of grace;
>> teach me to see in them thy loving purposes
>> and the joy and strength of my soul.

Thou hast prepared for me a feast;
   and though I am unworthy to sit down as a guest,
I wholly rest on the merits of Jesus,
   and hide myself beneath his righteousness;
When I hear his tender invitation
   and see his wondrous grace,
     I cannot hesitate, but must come to thee in love.
By thy Spirit enliven my faith rightly to discern
   and spiritually to apprehend the Saviour.
While I gaze upon the emblems of my Saviour's death,
   may I ponder why he died, and hear him say,
     'I gave my life to purchase yours,
      presented myself an offering to expiate your sin,
      shed my blood to blot out your guilt,
      opened my side to make you clean,
      endured your curses to set you free,
      bore your condemnation to satisfy divine justice.'
O may I rightly grasp the breadth and length of this
     design,
   draw near, obey, extend the hand, take the bread,
   receive the cup, eat and drink,
   testify before all men that I do for myself,
   gladly, in faith, reverence and love, receive my Lord,
   to be my life, strength, nourishment, joy, delight.
In the supper I remember his eternal love, boundless
     grace,
   infinite compassion, agony, cross, redemption,
   and receive assurance of pardon, adoption, life, glory.
As the outward elements nourish my body,
   so may thy indwelling Spirit invigorate my soul,
   until that day when I hunger and thirst no more,
   and sit with Jesus at his heavenly feast.

(From *The Valley of Vision*, a collection of Puritan prayers
                      and devotions).

Questions for discussion

1. If baptism is an individual's public declaration of faith in Christ, what is the Lord's Table? (1 Cor. 11:23-26). Who 'preaches' when the church eats the bread and drinks the wine?
2. The cup is called 'the cup of thanksgiving' (1 Cor. 10:16-17). What are we thankful for?
3. What care should God's people take in preparation for, and in the practice of, Holy Communion? (1 Cor. 11:17-34).
4. When Christ taught that we must 'eat his flesh and drink his blood', was his language to be understood literally or figuratively? (John 6:53-63).
5. Should professing Christians who persist in immoral living be admitted to the Lord's Table? (1 Cor. 5:9-11).

17.
Singing God's praise

Historically, Christians have been a singing people, and that is especially true of those denominations which share the heritage of the Protestant Reformation. Still, not all who profess faith in Christ are equally enthusiastic about music in the life of Christ's church. A friend once told me that he did not care much for the 'preliminaries'. He would have preferred to go directly to the sermon without any initial 'distractions'.

What does God's Word say about this matter? Are we under an obligation to sing? If so, why is this the case and what sort of songs are appropriate to the worship of God?

The new birth is a miracle of the grace of God. It is nothing less than the Holy Spirit coming to the rescue of a soul that is dead in trespasses and sins and imparting to that soul the life of God. Without regeneration no one can do anything in the Spirit. The unconverted man does not have the Spirit of God. He is devoid of any legitimate impulse to adore God. He may sing with the congregation of the redeemed, but he does not sing 'in the Spirit'. His worship is not acceptable to God.

But what of the converted man? Is his worship always acceptable? Is it possible for the regenerate man to fail in the practice of acceptable worship? Indeed it is. He must be filled with the Spirit of God; in other words his worship must be the product of his faith in the Lord (Eph. 5:18).

Why should we sing?

We serve a master who is King of kings and Lord of lords.
When he commands us we must obey. God's Word is filled
with commands that call for his worship and many of these
instruct his servants to sing his praises:

> Shout with joy to God, all the earth!
>   Sing the glory of his name;
>   make his praise glorious!
>
> (Ps. 66:1-2).

> Come and see what God has done,
>   how awesome his works on man's behalf!
>
> (Ps.66:5).

The psalmist recounts the great saving acts of God and
rightly calls us to worship. What greater motive is there for
musical praise than the character and works of God? We are
to sing because *the Lord is praiseworthy*.

Another reason for singing God's praise is that *it is good
for us*. Singing is a useful means of edification. Paul taught the
Ephesians to 'speak to one another with psalms, hymns, and
spiritual songs' (Eph. 5:19). We sing to the Lord but in doing
so we also speak to one another. By singing the great doctrines of the faith we build each other up in truth.

We also sing because it is the most appropriate way of *expressing the joy* we find in our Lord Jesus Christ. James taught
that a heart filled with joy should find a voice: 'Is anyone happy?
Let him sing songs of praise' (James 5:13).

What should we sing?

We have already said that the Bible commands us to sing
'psalms, hymns, and spiritual songs'. Just what is a hymn? In

classical Greek the word 'hymn' was used of a festive lyric written in praise of a god or hero. Therefore we understand that, when we use the word in the context of the Christian faith, we mean a song that is of non-biblical origin which none the less employs us in the direct praise of God. Such hymns are often overtly Christian, with Christ as the central subject of the song. Here is an example:

All hail the power of Jesus' name!
Let angels prostrate fall;
Bring forth the royal diadem,
And crown him Lord of all!

These words were crafted by Edward Perronet, in the eighteenth century, but they express truth that is grounded in the Word of God. In a day like ours, when subjectivism (the notion that we should be primarily concerned about our experience) and individualism (that truth is whatever I make it out to be) threaten to seduce much of the professing church, the singing of hymns provides a much-needed corrective. They point us to Christ as the one before whom we must bow in adoration. They remind us that this is the great goal of our journey. We are to be growing in the knowledge of God and in the ability to worship him well, for in fact we shall spend all of eternity doing just that.

This is not to say that we do not need songs about our experience. When the famous popular hymn-writer of the nineteenth century Fanny Crosby wrote about her experience of 'assurance' she was writing a spiritual song:

Blessed assurance, Jesus is mine!
Oh, what a foretaste of glory divine!
Heir of salvation, purchase of God,
Born of his Spirit, washed in his blood.

There is also a 'hymn book' that is divinely inspired. It is the Old Testament collection of songs that we know as the Book of Psalms. The word *psalmos*, as used by the apostle Paul in Ephesians 5:19, always denoted a song sung to musical accompaniment and was understood to refer specifically to psalms found in the Bible. It was inevitable therefore that the church should use the Psalter as its first hymnal and that it should model its hymns and spiritual songs on those found in the biblical book of Psalms.

Notice that I have referred to both hymns and spiritual songs as being represented in the book of Psalms. There we find, both songs that turn our thoughts God-ward and are useful as vehicles of praise, and songs that are about our experience as the redeemed people of God. Sometimes the two are mixed so that it is difficult to say where the impulse to praise the Lord ends, and the reflection on God's grace to us begins. A psalm of experience (spiritual song) would be Psalm 23. Here is a metrical (rhymed) version.

> The Lord's my Shepherd, I'll not want;
> He makes me down to lie,
> In pastures green he leadeth me
> The quiet waters by.

Psalm 100 is a psalm of praise (a hymn) and contains these lines:

> O enter then his gates with praise,
> Approach with joy his courts unto;
> Praise, laud and bless his name always,
> For it is seemly so to do.

> For why? The Lord our God is good,
> His mercy is for ever sure:

His truth at all times firmly stood,
And shall from age to age endure.

The singing of psalms is rare in churches today. A revival of psalmody in the churches would be very welcome indeed. Can we go on pretending that our worship is biblical if we do not sing psalms?

Worship or performance?

There is also another problem that must be addressed. It is what I call the 'show-business syndrome'. When I was a teenager, I attended a youth camp where young people were encouraged to 'give their testimony'. Camper after camper paraded to the microphone. Most of the 'testimonies' were primarily subjective in character but were sprinkled with pious-sounding sentiments. One little girl got caught up in the spirit of the thing and told us her life story minus the 'piety'. She saw people performing and jumped at the opportunity to take centre stage for herself.

Today there is little embarrassment about such behaviour. Many seminaries in America have 'music programs' that encourage the performance mentality. I recently visited a seminary chapel service. It was 'Reformation Day' and we could have been singing Martin Luther's *A Mighty Fortress Is Our God*, as well as other great hymns of the faith. That would have been appropriate. Instead, after presentations by a jazz ensemble and by singing groups, the congregation was invited to sing a couple of choruses with very little textual substance.

In many churches the 'audience' sits and is entertained by choirs and soloists. The 'audience' often expresses its appreciation by applause. If hymns are sung, few verses are used. 'Choruses' (which are not always to be despised) are preferred because they are short. The church that emphasizes the singing of psalms, hymns and spiritual songs by the congregation is a precious commodity in our day, but such churches do exist and the benefit to the congregation is enormous.

Finally, we need to show care in the choice of musical settings. A 'catchy' tune may be popular but inappropriate. Our God is a Sovereign of matchless dignity and therefore is worthy of our best offering. We may pander to popular taste and please man, but the worship that pleases the Lord is that which reflects his glory.

Questions for discussion

1. What songs are we to sing in the worship of God? (Eph. 5:19; Col. 3:16).
2. What are psalms, hymns and spiritual songs? How do they differ from each other?
3. According to Ephesians 5:19, to whom are we *speaking* when we sing?

18.
Prayer

In the Scriptures it is assumed that Christians will pray. It is also assumed that they need to be taught how to pray. Our Lord Jesus Christ included such instruction in his Sermon on the Mount. First, he warned his disciples about empty, hypocritical prayer: 'And when you pray, do not be like the hypocrites, for they love to pray standing in the synagogues and on the street corners to be seen by men. I tell you the truth, they have received their reward in full' (Matt. 6:5).

Our Lord reminded his hearers that God is unseen, and that he should be approached *without great public display*. Followers of Christ must seek a private place for communion with their God. They are to shut the door and in doing so to shut out the distractions of this world. Their praying will not be for the benefit of those who see them and are impressed with their piety. In the modern age the command of our Lord to shut the door is a bit more complicated than it was in the first century. It is not that we are in more danger of being pretentious than the early disciples of the Lord, but that there are more doors to shut than they ever dreamed of. Not only must we seek a place for prayer that is private, but the doors of our modern communication systems often have to be shut as well. I have learned, for example, that in order to have an uninterrupted time with the Lord as an individual, or with my family, I need not only to shut the door to the room or house where I intend to pray, but also take the telephone 'off the hook'.

The Lord also taught his disciples that prayer is *not a matter of many words*. Some people always seem to reason that more is better. That is not the case with prayer. There may be times when we will pray at length, even for hours. But mere repetition does not assure us that we shall be heard by the Lord or that we shall receive what we ask for. When I was a young man, I knew a man who, when asked to pray in church, always recited a long list of things that he wanted the Lord to know. I am certain that he was sincere in his practice but a bit misinformed. If one can pray with the understanding that the Lord already knows what we need, the praying will be less verbose. Our Lord said, 'And when you pray, do not keep on babbling like pagans, for they think they will be heard because of their many words. Do not be like them, for your Father knows what you need before you ask him' (Matt. 6:7-8).

What the Lord's Prayer teaches us

The Lord gave his disciples a model prayer, which has traditionally been called the Lord's Prayer. This prayer has been memorized and repeated thousands upon thousands of times, in private and in church services, down through the ages. It is good that this is so. But this prayer that the Lord gave to his people is a model. It was not intended *only* to be recited verbatim. It was intended to set before us the essential elements of prayer. We need to discover and use the fundamentals of prayer that were included in our Lord's teaching. What are these characteristics of true prayer?

The fatherhood of God

First, we are taught to approach God with a recognition of his fatherliness towards his people. One of the popular themes of eighteenth-century thought was the 'fatherhood of God, and the brotherhood of man'. God was seen as Creator of all things and therefore the 'Father' of all, and men were understood to be the result of God's highest creative act. As creatures of God, men are all brothers.

But this is not the meaning of our Lord. He taught that sin had separated men from their God and from one another. God is Father to those who have been saved by his grace. And there is a fellowship of believers which is a brotherhood transcending ethnic origin, nationality and status of any kind (Col. 3:11). It is the fellowship of those who have been redeemed by the blood of the Lamb.

The Lord did not teach us to pray, '*My* Father...' We may do so. We should do so. But when we pray, we should also remember that we were not saved to stand before God as redeemed individuals, but to be a part of God's family. When we pray, '*Our* Father...' we recall that the Lord is calling his people out from every nation and also from all of the ages. We have many brothers and sisters in Christ who are already with the Lord in heaven. We have many brothers and sisters in Christ here on the earth and our prayer reminds us that we have a responsibility of love towards them, as well as to God.

And God is our *Father.* He is '*Abba*'. He may be approached as a child would approach a good and loving father. He is the best of fathers, He will never fail us. He will always provide exactly the things that we need, both spiritual and material. He will not give us all that we ask for. He is a wise Father. Like a good earthly father, he will not grant requests, even though they may be sincere, if he knows that these would be harmful to us. A ten-year-old boy may ask his father for a fast car. No matter how much the boy pleads for it, a good father will not give his son something that is almost certain to harm him and others. God is such a Father. And he is not only wise, he is infinitely wise. He will never make a mistake. This should be the understanding that we have when we come before him. We should approach him with a recognition that his will is best for us.

A sense of God's transcendence

We also should approach the Lord with a sense of his transcendence. He is near to us. He is our Father. But he is also the true and living God who made all things. He is not of the earth. He dwells in heavenly splendour. He is our Father *in heaven.* Our Lord Jesus Christ has opened the way for us to enter into the very presence of God. The veil that separated men and women from the Holy of Holies in the temple has been torn apart. We may enter boldly into the very presence of our God. But this does not mean that we may enter God's presence in an offhand way. Our God is high and lifted up. He is King of kings. We bask in the intimacy of his love. But we must also remember that he is our God and worthy of our worship. In this century many Christians in the Western world have become very casual in their corporate worship. Because of this, it becomes an easy thing to forget that our God is in heaven. It is too easy to forget that he is holy.

This casual approach to the Lord is not the practice of Christians in many countries. While teaching in Russia, I discovered that the practice of Christians in that country is either to stand or kneel when praying. To sit while addressing God is thought to be inappropriate. It is, of course, the attitude of the heart that is paramount, but let us make certain that when we pray we remember that our God is in heaven and that he does whatever is pleasing to him. Let us remember that we are his creatures and that he is the one who made all things. Let us bow before him with a confidence that he will hear us and treat us as his children. Let us be assured that he will show love towards his own. And let us also remember to approach him as the God who reveals himself in the purity of holiness, into whose presence no sin can come, and who is worthy of worship from all of his creatures, especially those who have been saved by his grace.

God deserves our praise

And we are to recognize the holiness of 'the name' of the Lord. This is no mere concern for a particular pronunciation of the various names for God. This concerns the character of the Lord. It is the Lord who is perfect in righteousness. And that perfection has come down to earth in the Lord Jesus Christ. He bears the righteous character of his Father. He reveals the name or character of God because he is God.

Submission

We are also to pray for the success of the kingdom of God. We are to desire that his will should be honoured on earth just as it is in heaven. We must be willing to conform our own lives to his will. His command must be our clarion call to obedience. There is nothing that needs to take place on earth that is not included in the cry, 'Your kingdom come!' And there is nothing in our lives that should take place unless it may justly be included in that same petition. When we pray, 'Your kingdom come,' we are presenting ourselves before the throne of God and confessing our status as servants. We are reminding ourselves that we have been delivered from the kingdom of darkness into the kingdom of the eternal Son of God. We once served Satan, but now we belong to Christ and his will is our desire. We long to see his kingdom advance. We know that by his death and resurrection that kingdom has already prevailed and that its sure increase and final victory are assured.

Our petitions

The Lord also taught his disciples to seek 'daily bread' from the hand of God. When we pray for our daily bread we are praying for ordinary needs. We need food and clothing and shelter. Our God knows that we need such things but it is right and good for us to seek them from his hand. Thus we honour our heavenly Father as the giver of all things that are needed to sustain life.

But there is more implied in the request for daily bread. Our Lord Jesus Christ was born in a city (Bethlehem) whose name means 'house of bread'. And from the city of David, the house of bread, came one who is the Bread of Life. When we pray for daily nourishment, we should remember that the nourishment we need, more than any other, is the spiritual bread that has been given to us in Christ. Day by day, through faith, we feast on him. He is our true spiritual food.

Praying for forgiveness

We are also taught to pray for forgiveness. Our sins have been removed by Christ. We stand before God reconciled by the blood of Christ. We are said to be 'justified' by faith in him. But we have an inclination to sin that remains and we shall not be free of temptation and sin until we die, or until the day of Christ. We must examine our hearts to see if there is an unforgiving attitude towards others. We must examine our lives to see if we have truly forgiven those who have sinned against us. We must truly forgive before we come to God for forgiveness ourselves.

Praying for deliverance

Finally, in the Lord's Prayer, we are taught to pray for deliverance from times of trial. This is often translated 'temptation' because the hour of trial is here coupled with a request for deliverance from the Evil One. Only in eternity will we know how often the Lord has shown mercy to his children, when they have sought this blessing from him. There are times when the tempter must come. This was true in the life of our Lord Jesus Christ and we follow in his steps. But it is also right and good to pray for God's mercy in this matter. Let us pray that we shall not be led into a trial of our faith in which we are tempted. And let us remember that the apostle Paul said, 'No temptation has seized you except what is common to man. And God is faithful; he will not let you be tempted beyond what you can bear. But when you are tempted, he will also provide a way out so that you can stand up under it' (1 Cor. 10:13).

Other biblical teaching on prayer

The prayer that the Lord taught his disciples to pray contains petitions that can serve as our guide for prayer each day. And we are free to pray many prayers of different sorts. The Lord's prayer does not specifically mention thanksgiving, for example, but the Bible makes clear that it is right and good to give thanks to the Lord: 'And pray in the Spirit on all occasions with all kinds of prayers and requests' (Eph. 6:18).

Since prayer is an important part of our spiritual warfare with the forces of evil, we are to keep a clear head: 'With this in mind, be alert and always keep on praying for all the saints' (Eph. 6:18).

Notice that our prayers are to be directed to God 'for all the saints'. We are not only to pray for those Christian friends who are close to us and of whom we approve. We are to pray for all of God's people. We are to pray for their safety in a hostile world. But, most of all, we are to pray for them to grow in the truth that has been revealed in Christ and to become people who bring glory to God by the words they speak and by the life they live. We are to pray that they, with us, will become people who have it as our goal to love God fully and to love our fellow human beings as well. We are to pray that they and we will come to love as Christ has first loved us. We are to pray that the Holy Spirit will give us hearts that are full of the desire to follow Christ in humble service even to the undeserving.

Questions for discussion

1. How important are our motives in prayer? Should we be concerned about them? (Matt. 6:5).
2. Are long prayers especially pleasing to the Lord? (Matt. 6:7-8).
3. The Lord taught us to pray to 'our' Father. To whom was he referring when he used the word 'our'? (Col. 3:11).
4. What important elements of prayer were included by our Lord in the Lord's Prayer? How many can you identify? (Matt. 6:9-13).
5. Are we limited to praying only according to the model that the Lord gave us in the Sermon on the Mount? (Eph. 6:18).

19.
Living for Christ

Over the years many books have been written that claim to set forth the 'secret' of Christian living. A perusal of these volumes makes it clear that they do not agree as to what the essence of the Christian life really is. Many Christians have read various books with conflicting themes and then found themselves more confused than before.

Is there really a secret formula, or a particular experience, that opens the door to successful Christian living? Or is the answer to be found in the clearly expressed teaching of Holy Scripture?

There are three tenses of salvation. We look back to our *justification*. It was there that we first came to know the Lord Jesus Christ. We look ahead to future *glorification*. The day will come when all that we have known of sin will be but a memory. Perfect righteousness will not only be our possession in Christ, but will be ours in experience as well. But that time will only come when we no longer live in this present age. Our concern today is with the progressive work of the Lord on our behalf, which is called *sanctification*. We were justified by faith in Christ. We are being sanctified as he works out his salvation in us. And one day we shall stand before him glorified, having been made perfect by God's grace.

Christians are called 'saints' in the Bible. They are 'holy ones', for that is what the word 'saints' means. The Hebrew

word in the Old Testament that is translated 'holy' literally
means 'set apart'. Christians are people who have been set
apart by God's grace for his purpose. They are not called
'saints' because they are particularly pious, or because they
are known to be in heaven, as some teach. The designation
'saint' belongs to all who know Christ. They have been set
apart to new life in Christ, and that life is to be lived in a way
that is worthy of his gospel (Col. 1:10).

Three pitfalls to be avoided

In the quest for a holy life there are pitfalls to be avoided. The
apostle Paul warned the Colossians about three errors that
need to be avoided. The first was *legalism*. He told them to
resist letting anyone 'judge' them with regard to various requirements of the ceremonial law (Col. 2:16-17). These di-
etary restrictions and festivals for regular observance were
shadows of the truth that is now fully revealed in our Lord
Jesus Christ. We shall not become more acceptable to God
because we eat certain foods, or because we observe certain
religious rituals. The legalistic spirit calls us to a life where the
keeping of rules (often based, not on the Word of God, but on
the traditions of men) is seen as the essence of holy living.

Paul also warned against *mysticism* (Col. 2:18-19). Many
people make large claims that involve special revelations that
have come to them. They see 'visions', but their visions do
not harmonize with the clear teaching of the Bible. They seek
dramatic religious experiences. They are more concerned with
their own experience than with Christ and his person and work.

And the apostle identified *asceticism* as another spiritual
dead end. In the early centuries of Christendom some extrem-
ists sought holiness by separating themselves from society and
by a self-denial that involved treating their bodies very harshly.
The end result was supposed to be a mortification of the flesh

that would result in holiness of life. Religion for such people is defined by what you do not do. But Paul taught that this approach to Christian living has no value (Col. 2:20-23).

The Word of God as our standard for living

Where can we find a sure standard for living our lives? The Lord Jesus Christ met Satan's temptation with these words: 'It is written: "Man does not live on bread alone, but on every word that comes from the mouth of God"' (Matt. 4:4).

We need the whole counsel of God if we are to live in a way that is pleasing to him. That is not to say that a Christian cannot live for Christ until he or she has mastered all of the Scriptures. But it does mean that the revelation of God's will and way, which is ours in the Bible, is to be the standard of all that we think and do. We begin as babes in Christ, and the Lord in grace watches over us to keep us in the way. And as we are nourished by the truth of his Word, we grow in belief and practice. We should always remember that it is the Lord himself who is the central subject of the Bible and that his death and resurrection are the central truths upon which everything else depends. With that in mind, let us consider several things that are involved in living for Christ.

The law of God is our standard

Long ago the Lord met with Moses and the Israelites on Mount Sinai. There he gave them the 'Ten Words', or Commandments, that in past ages have been memorized by the children of believers as a part of their instruction in home, church and school. If we have been converted, we have experienced in some measure the evangelistic use of God's commandments. We must first discover that we are sinners. Sinners are people who have transgressed God's holy commandments. The Lord takes his standard of righteousness and stands us beside it. We, of course, are found to be wanting. And the Holy Spirit uses this to bring conviction to our hearts. We begin to feel the hot breath of God's law. We come to acknowledge our guilt. And, finally, we are brought to repent of our sin and cast ourselves on Christ for mercy. But does the law of God have a place in the life of believers?

The Sermon on the Mount (Matt. 5-7) is our Lord's exposition of God's law. And he preached that sermon to his disciples. He taught them that he did not come to abolish the law or the prophets (Matt. 5:17), but that he came to fulfil them. Christians today are to worship only the one true God, avoid idolatry, respect the name of God and keep the Sabbath holy. They are to show respect to their fathers and mothers and avoid murder, adultery, stealing, lying and covetousness. This is an enduring standard. And so it is good for Christians to meditate on the law of God. It is good for them to try to understand it better and to try to conform their lives to its requirements. The 119th psalm is a rhapsody on the theme of God's good and holy law from the perspective of a believer. We shall come to see the law of God as a lovely thing and worthy of day-long meditation (Ps. 119:97). We can then say with the psalmist,

> Your word is a lamp to my feet
>   and a light for my path.
> I have taken an oath and confirmed it
>   that I will follow your righteous laws
>
> (Ps. 119:105-106).

The very practical statement of our Lord, 'Do to others as you would have them do to you' (Luke 6:31), is merely a statement of the law in miniature.

The teaching of our Lord keeps us from the error of thinking that a mere outward keeping of the law will do. The Lord taught us that murderous or adulterous thoughts are tantamount to the act itself in the sight of God. We shall find ourselves in need of repentance again and again. We have not been made perfect yet. But our wills have been renewed and we now have the Holy Spirit dwelling within us. We can make progress. Our salvation is by grace, not by works. But that same salvation, if it is real, will produce good works done for the glory of God (Eph. 2:10).

We are to follow Christ as our example

In order for us to live in a way that pleases the Lord we must follow our Lord in *mortifying self*. Christ died for us and we must die to sin. We are to consider ourselves dead to sin but alive to Christ (Rom. 6:11). We are not to conform to this world, but to have our minds renewed in order to know and do God's will (Rom. 12:1-2). And we have been raised from spiritual death to new life in Christ. That new life is describable. We may define our new life by what is absent from it and by what is present there. By faith in Christ (dependence on his power), we learn to avoid sexual immorality, greediness, maliciousness, slandering the reputation of others, indecent stories, pride, lying and so on. All of these things, when examined, will be seen to be contrary to God's law. We learn how to see things a new way. Now we see all humanity as created in the image of God (Col. 3:10-11). We remember that the ground at the foot of the cross is level. We all had just one qualification for salvation — our need as sinners for forgiveness and justification.

As we seek to live for Christ, we will remember his *attitude*. He divested himself of heavenly splendour in order to condescend to us and to our need. He girded himself and washed his own disciples' feet. We shall no longer say, 'I demand my rights!' We shall no longer be primarily concerned with self-gratification, but with a desire to serve God and others. We shall hear the word of the Lord calling us to be compassionate, kind, humble, gentle and patient. We shall try with all our hearts to imitate the forgiving spirit of our Lord. He forgave us when we were undeserving and, as we remember this, we shall not qualify our forgiveness by requiring of others what the Lord has not required of us.

Our lives as an act of worship

The life of holiness is itself an act of worship. We are to be filled with thankfulness for the greatness of the salvation that is ours in Christ (Eph. 5:19-20). We no longer have a ministry that is performed before an altar of stone with bloody sacrifices, but we do offer up spiritual sacrifices as we praise God and as we do works of mercy in his name (Heb. 13:15-16). We have a contribution to make to the local assembly of believers. We serve God by our faithful presence in the meetings of his church (Heb. 10:25). We serve God by setting apart a generous portion of our income to support the men that God has called to teach us his Word, to help the poor and to help others carry the gospel message to the ends of the earth.

Our family relationships

The Christian's family relationships must be pleasing to the Lord (Eph. 5:22 - 6:4) In fact, every relationship must be approached from the vantage-point of service. We are called to submit to others. The Lord taught us that to be great in the kingdom of God is to become a servant. We must not first ask, 'What is in this for me?' but 'How can I seek the good of others?' even at great cost to myself. That price may be paid in money, time, emotional strain, or in various other ways. But we must not shrink from it. Our Lord was willing to do much more. He was willing to die in the place of the undeserving. Christian fathers will love their wives as Christ loved the church. Remember that our Lord laid down his life for his church. And they will take the responsibility for teaching their wives and children the basic principles of holy living. They will not shirk the duty of leading the family that the Lord has entrusted to their care. And they will do this, not by word alone, but by example as well.

The Christian and the state

We also have the responsibility of living as citizens of the heavenly kingdom in a world that is not at all a heavenly place. We cannot plead exemption from duties that are laid upon us by the nation in which we live. Every Christian has a dual citizenship. We may be Canadian, or Russian, or Japanese, but we are also members of Christ's body and citizens of his kingdom. We must pay taxes to the earthly government. We must obey the laws of the land. There are actually very few times when Christians are called upon to disobey such laws. By living as good citizens we honour not only the earthly authorities, but our God as well (Rom. 13:1-7).

It is important to understand the priority of God's kingdom in our lives. Near my home there is a church that has three flag-poles in its grounds. On one a flag representing Christianity is displayed, and on another the flag of our state. These two flags fly on poles which are the same in height. In the centre is the national flag. It is on a higher level than the other two. What is thus symbolized is regrettable. No earthly nation should have the place of honour that is to be reserved for our God and for his kingdom.

The time may come when a choice will have to be made between serving God and obeying man. The authorities commanded Peter and John not to teach in the name of Jesus. Their reply was: 'Judge for yourselves whether it is right in God's sight to obey you rather than God. For we cannot help speaking about what we have seen and heard' (Acts 4:19-20).

I once spoke in a church whose first thirteen pastors had been imprisoned, from ten to twenty-five years, for their loyalty to Christ. All but two of them died in the labour camps. Most Christians are not called upon to make such a sacrifice, but if the providence of the Lord leads us down the path of persecution, he will provide the grace we need.

Our response to ill-treatment

If we suffer ill-treatment how are we to respond? We are to avoid repaying evil with evil. We are to live at peace with everyone as far as it depends on us. We are to feed our enemies if they are hungry. There is also evangelistic value in holy living. Peter said, 'Live such good lives among the pagans that, though they accuse you of doing wrong, they may see your good deeds and glorify God on the day he visits us' (1 Peter 2:12).

Because Christ suffered for us and left us an example of how to live, when we are insulted, we will not retaliate; when suffering wrongly, we will not threaten those who mistreat us. In this way, we will bring glory to God and good to ourselves as we grow in true holiness of life.

Our active participation in the process of sanctification

Have you noticed that in all of this we are very much engaged as active participants? It is error to think that we shall grow in sanctification by simply trying to be as passive as possible. Some have taught that this is the way to a 'higher life'. But the language and images of Scripture give the lie to this approach. We are to think of ourselves as soldiers in the army of God. We are to put on the whole armour of God (Eph. 6:10-18). We are to be actively engaged against the enemies of God. We are told to resist the devil. We are to use the redeemed faculties that God has given us. And we are encouraged to persevere when we learn that the one who is 'in' us is greater than 'the one who is in the world' (1 John 4:4). It is certainly true that it is God who is at work in us. It is also true that we must 'work out' our salvation with 'fear and trembling' (Phil. 2:12-13).

When we stand before the Lord, we shall be bound to admit that we have been saved only by his grace. And we shall give all the glory to him for anything good that has been done in his name. But we must not use that as an excuse for spiritual laziness.

Questions for discussion

1. What three pitfalls did the apostle Paul warn us about in Colossians 2:16-23?
2. Can any biblical doctrine be dismissed as unimportant, in the process of sanctification? (Matt. 4:4).
3. Where can we find our Lord's own exposition of the law of God?
4. What statement of our Lord sums up the law of God? (Luke 6:31).
5. According to Colossians 3:1-17, what things are we to put off, and what things are we to put on?
6. What is the biblical principle of submission, and what is its connection to Christian living?
7. What is our responsibility to the nation in which we live? (Rom. 13:1-7).
8. What should we do if the commandment of God and the laws of men do not agree? (Acts 4:18-20).

20.
The return of our Lord

There are a number of very questionable (but very popular) doctrines that are taught as essential to the Christian's understanding of the future. It is my judgement that these 'essentials' are really the opinions of men, which have been superimposed on what God's Word actually teaches concerning the return of the Lord.

Some see the Bible as a map of all future events, including the particulars of each nation's history. In recent years, many have taught that the key to understanding the future, as it is set forth in the Bible, is the nation of Israel. They assume that God is concerned, first and foremost, with national (racial) Israel, and that all other works of God are subsumed under that concern, including God's purposes for his church. Thus, when many Christians hear rumours about the possible rebuilding of the temple at Jerusalem they are excited by the prospect that the return of the Lord is growing near. They envisage a return in which the Lord will come to a literal temple and establish a reign from there that will reveal his sovereignty over the nations.

Thousands of evangelical Christians have heard sermons, and even viewed motion pictures, which depict an end-time catastrophe complete with planes falling from the sky and family members disappearing (having been secretly snatched away), while those who do not know Christ are left behind to wonder what has taken place. Are these things indeed taught in Scripture, or is this mere conjecture?

Such speculation is not limited to Christians and sometimes provides a bit of humour. Recently, while on a long transoceanic flight, I sat next to a Jewish man who was reading his Bible. He was happy to find a travelling companion who could read Hebrew and with whom he could converse on matters suitable for the Sabbath day. I had the opportunity to explain the gospel of Christ to him, and in the course of our conversation, we talked about various Jewish groups, and the differences in their doctrines and practices. As we approached our destination (New York), he told me about a group of 'orthodox' Jews in the New York City area who have begun to carry pagers wherever they go. They are convinced that the Messiah will soon come and that he will make his appearing known to certain of their leaders, who then will give them a call to let them know that the Messiah has arrived.

Among Christians, from time to time, some new teacher arises who claims to know the hour of the Lord's return. Not a few gullible folks have sat on a hillside, or gathered in a room together, to await the sure return of the Lord. In the last decade a book was published which claimed to be able to pinpoint the time of Christ's return. Such volumes often bring thousands of dollars to the bank accounts of their authors, even though they are soon demonstrated to be in error.

Not long ago, a group of people moved from Taiwan to Garland, Texas, because Garland (they say) sounds like 'God's land'. Their leader set a date for the Lord to appear. The date passed. The end had not yet come.

Where can truth be found? We must again go 'to the law and to the testimony' (see Isa. 8:20). Only in the Word of God can we find the truth concerning the return of Christ and our future with him.

What can we say about the Second Coming of Christ and the future of his people and be confident that we are on a firm biblical foundation? Let me suggest several truths that will give us a good basic understanding of eschatology or, as it is sometimes called, the doctrine of the last things.

The time of his coming is unknown

Nothing that happens at the coming of the Lord will overshadow the accomplishment of his first advent. When the Lord first appeared on the earth almost two thousand years ago, he came to establish God's kingdom in perfection. He came to bring righteousness to the earth in a way that had never been known before. He came to bring a new and better work of the Holy Spirit to the hearts of those who would believe. He came to bring God's eternal life to the people of God. All these things were accomplished by his death and resurrection. He is reigning above and interceding for his own. The battle for the souls of God's elect people is proceeding and Christ is going forth to conquer the foe. Satan's power has been broken. His doom is sure. The return of our Lord will bring to fulfilment all of the things that were won by his death and resurrection. But *the time of the Lord's return is unknown*. Our Lord taught his disciples, 'No one knows about that day or hour, not even the angels in heaven, nor the Son, but only the Father' (Matt. 24:36).

When you hear of someone who claims to be able to predict the time of the Lord's appearing, you may write that person off as a charlatan, or at best as being very confused. No one knows the time of Christ's return. You may say, 'But didn't the Lord speak about earthquakes and famines and wars and rumours of wars that would take place just prior to his return? Aren't there signs that we can look for?' The Lord did speak of earthquakes and famine and wars and rumours of wars, but specifically warned us not to be alarmed. These were not signs of the *end*, but of the *beginning* and of the sure proclamation of the gospel to all the nations (Matt. 24:1-14). The truth is that only God knows the time of the return of Christ.

The need to be ready

The Lord will come at an hour which will be characterized by *its normality*. He taught that the time of his return would find the people of this world doing the things that they were doing when the flood of Noah came upon them 'and took them all away' (Matt. 24:37-40). They were eating and drinking and marrying and giving in marriage (all normal human behaviour). They did these things right up to the time when Noah and his family boarded the ark. They did not expect the judgement of God to fall on them. They would go on doing the things that human beings do, and there would be no accountability for sin — so they thought.

The Lord gave this example: 'Two men will be in the field; one will be taken and the other left. Two women will be grinding with a hand mill; one will be taken and the other left' (Matt. 24:41). Just as the wicked people of Noah's time were 'taken away' to judgement by the flood, so the coming of our Lord will divide humanity into two parts — those who are taken away to judgement and those who are not. May we not be among those who are taken away! We are to be prepared at all times: 'Therefore, keep watch, because you do not know on what day your Lord will come' (Matt. 24:42).

The Bible teaches *the imminent return of Christ*. We are not taught to think that we have a lot of time to spare. He may not come today, but we do not know that. We must not think that there are so many things to be fulfilled before his return

that we may rest for a while. We do not know when he will
return, and we must be ready. The Lord taught several para-
bles which emphasize this truth. He spoke about the master of
a house who went away to a wedding banquet. His servants
were expected to be alert and ready to open the door *immediately* on his return (Luke 12:35-40). On another occasion he
spoke about the owner of a house who would in time close the
door of the house. Those outside would knock and plead with
him but he would tell them, 'I don't know you or where you
come from' (Luke 13:22-30).

It will be a physical, visible return

The Lord will return in bodily form. Luke gave us an account
of the ascension of the Lord after his resurrection from the
dead. The Lord was taken up into heaven before the eyes of
his apostles and hidden from their sight by a cloud. Two 'men'
dressed in white appeared and spoke to the apostles in this
way: 'Men of Galilee ... why do you stand here looking into
the sky? This same Jesus, who has been taken from you into
heaven, will come back in the same way you have seen him go
into heaven' (Acts 1:9-11).

The clear teaching is this: our Lord ascended bodily and
was concealed from sight; one day he will be revealed again in
bodily form and will descend from above. Some may protest
by asking how he can be seen by all if he is to return in his
glorified body. With God all things are possible.

The church will be reunited

The Second Coming of Christ will also bring about a union of
the church militant and the church triumphant. One of the oldest

confessions of faith speaks of the 'communion of saints'. This is not merely a reference to the fellowship of living Christians, but includes the common experience of salvation through Christ, which is shared by the living and the dead. Thousands who came to faith in Christ while living here on the earth are now with the Lord. They live in heaven with him and are far better off for it. They have traditionally been called 'the church triumphant' while those who are still here in this world are thought of as 'the church militant', the church on the march against the forces of evil here below.

Revelation 7 gives us a symbolic picture of the church militant (and under the protection of the Lord) in verses 1-8 and the church triumphant in verses 9-17. We are all one in Christ and have a common communion now, but at the return of our Lord what we now experience by faith will have become sight. The Bible teaches us that the church triumphant will return with our Lord: 'We believe that Jesus died and rose again and so we believe that God will bring with Jesus those who have fallen asleep in him. According to the Lord's own word, we tell you that we who are still alive, who are left till the coming of the Lord, will certainly not precede those who have fallen asleep. For the Lord himself will come down from heaven, with a loud command, with the voice of the archangel and with the trumpet call of God, and the dead in Christ will rise first. After that, we who are still alive and are left will be caught up together with them in the clouds to meet the Lord in the air. And so we will be with the Lord for ever' (1 Thess. 4:14-17).

A public event

This very important passage teaches us that the return of Christ will not be a hidden event. There will be a loud command, the voice of the archangel will be heard and the trumpet call of God will sound. The notion of a secret rapture, or catching up of the church, is not taught in the Scriptures. The Second Coming will be a noisy event. One cannot miss it. All people will know that Christ our Lord has returned. Christians will rejoice, but the lost will be terrified because of their sins and the judgement to come.

The resurrection of the dead

As we have seen, the dead will be raised. This is true of both the righteous and the unrighteous. Once during a discussion about the doctrine of last things, I commented that both the righteous and the wicked would be raised from the dead. Someone asked me, wherever did I get such an idea? It was, of course, our Lord himself who taught this: 'Do not be amazed at this, for a time is coming when all who are in their graves will hear his voice and come out — those who have done good will rise to live, and those who have done evil will rise to be condemned' (John 5:28-29).

The Lord did not call the experience of the resurrected unbelievers 'life'. Only the righteous really 'live'. The wicked exist in a state of eternal torment. Hell becomes their dwelling-place for ever. But all the dead will be raised. The Bible does not give us much information concerning the bodily existence of those who are eternally lost. But there is quite a bit of information concerning the future state of the redeemed. Since we shall be 'like Christ', it is instructive to remember that he even ate with his disciples after he had been resurrected from the dead. Our existence will not be a shadowy matter, but the reality of our life in that new day will be, if anything, far more *real* than life in this world. And our new body will be one that is designed for perfect fellowship with our God. All sin will then be past. Mortality (which is the result of sin) will then also be a thing of the past. The immortal life of God will be ours in truth. As Paul said, we shall 'bear the likeness of the man from heaven' (1 Cor. 15:49).

The final judgement

The return of our Lord will also bring in the final judgement of God, which will be a judgement based on principles of righteousness. The Scriptures teach us that all must face this judgement: 'For we must all appear before the judgement seat of Christ, that each one may receive what is due to him for the things done while in the body, whether good or bad' (2 Cor. 5:10).

Those who try to stand before the righteous Judge in that day without the grace of God to shield them will only know the wrath of the Lamb of God. Their sins will be judged and their 'righteous acts' will be shown to be nothing more than filthy rags in the sight of God. Those who know Christ will also be judged on principles of righteousness, but will have the continuing intercession of the Son of God. They will be shown mercy for their sins, and their works which were done as the result of the indwelling of God's Holy Spirit will be recognized as pure and acceptable in the sight of God.

Scoffers will always appear to deny the truth that Christ will come again. Peter put it this way: 'First of all, you must understand that ... scoffers will come, scoffing and following their own evil desires. They will say, "Where is this 'coming' he promised? Ever since our fathers died, everything goes on as it has since the beginning of creation"' (2 Peter 3:3-4).

Peter also taught the certainty of final judgement, and that the Lord cannot be rightfully accused of not keeping his promises: 'But do not forget this one thing, dear friends: With the

Lord a day is like a thousand years, and a thousand years are like a day' (2 Peter 3:8). Our God dwells in eternity. He is the Creator of time and space. His perspective on these things is far superior to ours. He is patient with sinners but the time will come for his return.

The new heavens and new earth

The return of our Lord will mean the end of the universe and the revelation of a new heaven and a new earth. The apostle Peter also taught that the present order of things is to come to an end. The old creation has been spoiled by Adam's fall and the sins of subsequent generations. It must and will be replaced. A new creation has already come in Christ. The death and resurrection of our Lord brought in a new and perfect order. That new order has been advancing against the forces of evil for many years. One day the Lord himself will return and we shall see the unveiling of Christ's perfection and the glorious character of his kingdom. That kingdom will displace all others. We may love the country in which we were born. We may be strongly patriotic. But the mature Christian comes to understand that our citizenship is really heavenly; we are first and foremost citizens of God's kingdom and it is the only kingdom that will endure for all eternity. We should long to see the nations pass away and to see Christ's kingdom come. It is not national Israel that God is ultimately concerned about but the true Israel, which is spiritual. The true Israel is the church of the living God. She is the holy nation (1 Peter 2:9).

And there will no longer be a great divide between heaven and earth (Rev. 21:1). In other words, the dwelling-place of God and the dwelling-place of man will have been brought together by the graciousness of our God. In a sense, we shall dwell on the earth for ever. Earth, our dwelling-place, will have been created new, and there will be no essential difference between heaven and earth. But the significant thing is that we shall be able to live in the very presence of our God because we shall have been brought to perfection ourselves. We were once justified before God in spite of our sins because of God's grace given us in Christ. We were sanctified by the continuing work of God in us over the years of our lives. But in that day we shall be glorified.

We shall know the perfection of absolute holiness. We shall truly be righteous as our Lord is righteous. There will be no more tears (Rev. 21:4) There will be no more sin (Rev. 21:8). The same passage teaches that Christ will have made his church splendid in holiness. The figures of this passage do not describe the literal streets of heaven; they set before us the splendours of the church in all of her redeemed glory. We are told that we shall have entered an eternal day. Light is a symbol of truth and righteousness in Scripture. There will be no need for the sun. We shall have the light of God's presence for ever. And there will be perfect joy and satisfaction. We shall drink of the water of life. Now to be sure, this is highly symbolic language. But the symbols stand for reality, a reality that we shall only begin to understand when we begin to experience it. We shall enjoy our God, and enjoy one another, for ever. His fellowship will be immediate to us, and all the things that mar our present fellowship with our brothers and sisters in Christ will be forgotten.

In that glorious eternal day we shall sing with those who went before us the song of Revelation 5:12-13:

To him who sits on the throne and to the Lamb
be praise and honour and glory and power,
        for ever and ever!

We do not know when our Lord will appear. We are commanded to wait patiently for his appearing. We are to trust him for all things. We are to trust him day by day. And, by

God's grace, we may from time to time glimpse our future blessings. The time will come when we must stand on this side of the 'Jordan'. We must pass through the 'valley of the shadow of death'. And beyond awaits glory and blessing which we can only imagine now. In the words of the hymn by Samuel Stennett we say:

On Jordan's stormy banks I stand,
And cast a wishful eye
To Canaan's fair and happy land
Where my possessions lie.

Oh, the transporting, rapturous scene
That rises to my sight!
Sweet fields arrayed in living green,
And rivers of delight.

O'er all those wide extended plains
Shines one eternal day:
There God the Son for ever reigns,
And scatters night away.

When shall I reach that happy place,
And be for ever blest?
When shall I see my Father's face,
And in his bosom rest?

Dear reader, it is the desire of God's children to be with the Lord. Is that true of your heart? Do you long for his appearing? Do you hope for an eternity with him? Do you believe that his promises are true? Has he changed your heart from a love of sin to love for him, and for his people?

Are you trusting in Christ alone for pardon, and for deliverance in the great Day of Judgement? Are you ready to meet your God?

Questions for discussion

1. What is the relationship between the first appearance of Christ and his second coming?

2. Can anyone know the time of the return of Christ? (Matt. 24:36-42).

3. Will the Lord return in bodily fashion? Shall we be able to see him? (Acts 1:9-11).

4. What about those who have died in the Lord? What part will they play in the return of Christ? Will his return be a public event, or will he come secretly? (1 Thess. 4:14-17).

5. What will eternity be like for those who are in Christ? (Rev. 21-22).

Index